WICKED ALBANY

WICKED ALBANY

LAWLESSNESS & LIQUOR
IN THE PROHIBITION ERA

frankie y. bailey and **alice p. green**

Charleston · London

THE
History
PRESS

Published by The History Press
Charleston, SC 29403
www.historypress.net

Copyright © 2009 by Frankie Y. Bailey and Alice P. Green
All rights reserved

First published 2009

Manufactured in the United States

ISBN 978.1.59629.493.6

Library of Congress Cataloging-in-Publication Data
Bailey, Frankie Y.
Wicked Albany : lawlessness and liquor in the Prohibition era / Frankie Y. Bailey and Alice
P. Green.
p. cm.
Includes bibliographical references.
ISBN 978-1-59629-493-6
1. Prohibition--New York (State)--Albany--History--20th century. 2. Albany (N.Y.)--Social
conditions--20th century. I. Green, Alice P., 1946- II. Title.
HV5090.N7B35 2009
364.109747'4309042--dc22
                                    2008047472

CONTENTS

PREFACE

Those readers who have experience with historical research will know that there is always more than one version of any event. Even the most mundane happening is subject to interpretation by the observers of the event and those who write about it later. When it comes to crime and Prohibition-era politics, this is certainly the case.

We have based this book on the works of local historians (including academic theses and dissertations on specific topics), newspaper coverage, annual police reports, police scrapbooks (containing newspaper crime reports) and other documents about the Prohibition era. We have tried to be as factual as possible, offering the best version of the "facts" as we were able to uncover them. We acknowledge in advance that we, too, have interpreted what we found, and there are certainly other stories that could and should be told.

We should also note here that minor variations in names of local establishments (e.g., hotels) may appear in the text. This is because we have followed the form used in our sources, which were not always consistent, and because names did occasionally change.

ACKNOWLEDGEMENTS

We would like to thank the many people who provided help and encouragement as we worked on this book. We apologize in advance to anyone whose name we forget to mention here. As with many books, this one came to life through the contributions of numerous people other than the authors.

First, we would like to thank the staff of the Albany County Hall of Records, including Deputy Director Craig Carlson, Jill Hughes, Jimmy Farinacci, John Paul Ciejka and Eric Phoenix. We are especially grateful for the police scrapbooks (containing newspaper clippings about crime in Albany), the photographs, the special Legs Diamond collection, the Common Council annual police reports and the other archival materials available at the Hall of Records.

We want to thank Ellen Gamache and Christopher Sagaas at the Albany Public Library; Monica Bartoszek and the other members of the staff at the *Times-Union*; and Allison Munsell at the Albany Institute of History and Art. They all provided us with invaluable assistance in finding and processing the photos included in this book. We also want to express our gratitude to James Atkins of the New York State Police Planning and Research Section, who provided us with photos from the State Police archives that we would not have been able to find elsewhere.

Our gratitude also to Mike Spain, associate editor at the *Times-Union*, who provided the answer to a question about Albany newspaper chronology and directed us to a useful historical link.

We would like to thank Detective James Miller, Public Information Office, and Lieutenant Howard Schechter, Forensics Unit, of the Albany Police

ACKNOWLEDGEMENTS

Department. Detective Miller referred us to Lieutenant Schechter, who was able to solve for us the mystery of the geographic location of the "precincts" in the 1920s and 1930s (which were not the same as the current "divisions" of the Albany Police Department) and who kindly shared Albany history documents in his collection.

We would like to thank New York State Assemblyman Jack McEneny, Albany historian and author of *Albany: Capital City on the Hudson*, who took the time from his busy schedule to chat with us about Albany history. We also would like to thank William Kennedy for his novels about Albany in the 1930s and his informal history, *O, Albany!*

We would like to thank Mrs. Lila Touhey, who provided us with a book of photos of Old Albany and her encouragement.

We would like to thank Kristen Smith, who worked at the Center for Law and Justice and who is now a PhD student in the Sociology Department, University at Albany, for her incredibly efficient assistance.

Frankie would like to thank the students who were in her Spring 2008 Historical Research Methods seminar in the School of Criminal Justice, University at Albany, for listening to her Albany stories and inspiring her by the way they dived into their own research projects.

Finally, we both want to thank Melissa Schwefel, former editor at The History Press, who invited us to do this project. Most of all, we want to thank our editor, John Wilkinson, who was both patient and just plain nice as we went through the process of turning a manuscript into a book.

Chapter 1

1919

On August 19, 1919, the *Times-Union*, an Albany, New York newspaper, carried a front-page story titled "Insulted, Girl Beats One Man, Routs His Pals." According to the reporter, a female cyclist, clad in the short skirts that women wore for this activity, was riding her bicycle when she became the object of vulgar remarks from male "bench warmers" in Townsend Park. Her "feminine dignity" outraged, the young woman curbed her bicycle and marched over to confront the "loafers." She slapped the face of the man who had spoken first and followed with several jabs to his body. Stunned by this onslaught, the man and his friends beat a hasty retreat. As they ran, the young woman called after them, "I'll show you hoboes whether I'm a lady—" and invited them to return if they wanted some more of the same. They did not. The young woman retrieved her bicycle and pedaled away, heading west.[1]

This episode captures varied aspects of American life in 1919. Clad in a short skirt and out alone on her bicycle, the young woman defended her own honor when insulted by vulgar males. Representative of the "New Woman" who had appeared in the late nineteenth century, she was vigorous, not retiring. She demanded respect. She symbolized the debate going on, even among women themselves, about "fashion reform" that would allow a woman to wear clothing that was comfortable and suitable for the activity in which she was engaged. Another matter of debate in periodicals was whether bicycle riding was healthy for young women.

No longer confined to a "bicycle built for two" shared with a male companion, the female cyclist could now pedal away under her own power on a "safety bicycle."[2] She had gained two-wheeled mobility. In this regard, the young woman on her bicycle had something in common with the rowdy men in the park. The reporter described the men as "loafers," but the young woman called them "hoboes." Since the nineteenth century, "hoboes" had been "riding the rails" aboard the trains that connected the country from east to west. The varied reputation of these vagabond travelers reflected the fears and needs of other less mobile Americans. In their day, hoboes had been described as useless bums who should be chased out of town or predatory strangers who should be arrested. But in some places, they had been welcomed as migrants who provided the temporary labor needed to harvest crops. In the early twentieth century, books and stories by authors such as Jack London had made hoboes romantic figures in the imaginations of those who longed to take to "the open road."[3]

The hoboes lounging in the park that day in Albany struck both the young woman and the reporter as "slackers." As World War I ended, able-bodied men were expected either to be in military uniform or holding down a job on the homefront. Instead, these men were engaged in the kind of unruly male behavior in public places that had troubled respectable urban dwellers since the birth of the modern city. On that August day in 1919, when "New Woman" confronted "loafers" and a reporter recorded the incident for the consumption of a newspaper audience, Albany, the capital city of New York State, was like the rest of the country. Albany had one foot in the prewar past and one foot in the next decade, when much about American life and culture would change.

Already, young Americans born after 1900 were experiencing technological wonders that would have amazed their grandparents born before or just after the Civil War. By the 1920s, Americans would be able to listen to World Series baseball games on the radio. Between the two World Wars, even those Americans living in the rural countryside would acquire a radio window onto the world. For city dwellers, the speed of change was reflected in the array of merchandise displayed in department store windows. And there were those gleaming, new automobiles. Bicycles were fine for leisure, but the automobile now allowed Americans to cover greater distances—or it would, as soon as the "good roads movement" underway across the country provided the paved roads that would make it possible to drive outside the city without dealing with ruts, mud and other hazards. Already there was a sense of the possibilities that the automobile would offer.

In 1919, Albany and America teetered on the brink of the discordant "jazz age" that would feature Prohibition lawbreaking and the economic boom and bust that would plunge the country into the Great Depression.

North Pearl Street between Steuben and Maiden Lane. Note the Albany Theatre and the variety of shops and other businesses. *Courtesy of Albany Public Library.*

Pearl Street (north), East Side, looking south from Orange Street. Note the prices and the display of fresh produce. *Courtesy of Albany Public Library.*

WICKED ALBANY

Politics and Crime

That year in Albany, some things remained the same. Like a number of other American cities, including Chicago and New York City, Albany was run by a "political machine." Born in the wards of the nineteenth-century city, political machines were characterized by the dominance of a single party, which controlled both the municipal government and the patronage "plums" (jobs and positions) distributed to supporters of the party. In 1919, the reigning political machine in Albany was Republican. William "Billy" Barnes, well-educated and well-to-do, was the Republican leader ("boss" according to his political enemies). Barnes was the grandson of Thurlow Weed, politician and founder of a local newspaper, the *Albany Evening Journal*. Barnes had inherited the newspaper from his grandfather.

Former governor and Democrat Martin H. Glynn, one of the Republican machine's harshest critics, owned a rival Albany newspaper, the *Times-Union*. Since the birth of journalism in America, newspapers had taken sides in political battles. Even as the *New York Times* and other major newspapers strove for "professionalism" and "objective reporting," early twentieth-century politics affected what was reported by the press. This was particularly the case when the politician owned a newspaper. Born in Valatie, New York, a small town in Columbia County, Glynn was the son of a saloon owner. He personified the hard work followed by upward mobility that was the essence of the American dream. He had attended Fordham University and passed the bar exam to practice law but instead became a journalist. With the help of a Fordham classmate, Glynn obtained a position at the *Times-Union* and eventually became the editor, publisher and owner of the newspaper.[4]

In 1899, Glynn was elected to the United States Congress. He went on to serve as New York State comptroller and as the lieutenant governor in William Sulzer's administration. When Sulzer was impeached, Glynn became the first Roman Catholic governor of New York (1913–14). Even while holding public office, Glynn retained control of the *Times-Union*. When he was once again a private citizen, he focused his energies on running the newspaper. In 1919, as a mayoral election approached, Glynn's newspaper challenged what Democrats in Albany described as the corrupt Republican machine. In the months leading up to the election, the *Times-Union* waged a relentless attack on the handling of city government by Mayor James R. Watt, Commissioner of Public Safety J. Sheldon Frost and Corporation Counsel Arthur L. Andrews.

Such attacks on the Barnes Republican machine were not new. In 1911, Albany city and county officials had been the focus of what was called "the

Albany Inquiry." Comparing the inquiry to the probe into New York City police corruption by the 1890s' Lexow Committee, the *New York Times* called it "'Lexowing' Albany."[5] In Albany, one focus of the inquiry was alleged no-bid contracts, including the arrangement between the state and J.B. Lyon Printing (a company in which Barnes had a financial interest). The second focus of the inquiry was the reported existence of a "red light district" in Albany, where "vice" activities, including gambling and prostitution, went on undeterred by the local police department.[6]

The investigation included a dramatic confrontation between James W. Osborne, the Committee's counsel, and William Barnes, who was called to testify before the Senate Committee. Barnes frustrated Osborne's attempt to question him about the activities of a secretive group called the "Lincoln League," which Osborne believed was an arm of the Republican Party. Barnes also refused to answer Osborne's questions about Barnes's own business activities or to provide the business records sought by the Committee.[7] When he was ordered to cooperate by a lower court judge, Barnes petitioned to be heard before the New York State Court of Appeals. He won his appeal.[8]

Deprived of information from Barnes, the Committee ended its inquiry and delivered its report to the New York State Senate. The report was first rejected on a technicality concerning whether or not the Committee's term had expired. After political brokering between Democrats and Republicans, the report was accepted.[9] The submitted report was blistering in its charges of neglect of duty and corruption by Albany officials. The Committee offered a lengthy description of Albany's "red light district" (known as "the Gut"). Much of this information was gathered by Robert McClellan, a former detective who had gone to Albany and attempted to open a disorderly house (house of prostitution and/or other vice activities). McClellan had encountered no difficulty in doing this. He had even received advice on finding women to staff the house from the Republican district leader (who was also employed at the county jail). The Committee described a general pattern of corruption by Republican officials in Albany linked to the Barnes political machine. Mayor James B. McEwan and Commissioner of Public Safety E.B. Cantine were, the Committee said, practicing "a settled policy of segregation of vice." At the same time, all forms of gambling were going on unchecked in both the city and county of Albany. William Barnes dismissed both the Committee's inquiry and its report. He argued, with perhaps some truth, that the inquiry had been instigated by his political enemy, Albany Democratic boss Paddy McCabe.[10]

By 1919, William Barnes had alienated some fellow Republicans[11] with a style of leadership that was occasionally arrogant and by his position on some issues (he opposed Prohibition). Still, Barnes's machine remained formidable enough to engage in a hard-fought battle as the 1919 election approached. The partisan newspapers owned by Barnes and Martin Glynn played a major role in that battle, providing each side with daily access to Albanians.

Women in the state had won the right to vote in 1917, and each political party appealed to the female voters of Albany. Less than a week before the election, Glynn's *Times-Union* featured a front-page editorial cartoon with the caption, "The Barnes Machine 'Smashed' the Women of Albany in 1917—The Women of Albany Will 'Smash' the Barnes Machine in 1919."[12] This was a reference to opposition and lack of support for women's suffrage by Republican politicians. The newspaper also suggested that women should be vexed by Mayor Watt's failure to provide requested funds for the celebration that the women of Albany wanted to hold for returning soldiers. Additionally, the mayor had not attended the dinner given by the women in the veterans' honor and to which he had been invited. The newspaper predicted that the women would exact their revenge by voting for Democratic candidates. The *Times-Union* assured female readers that they could be confident that by overthrowing the Barnes machine they would be fighting corruption.

Earlier that month, Barnes's *Albany Evening Journal* had made its own appeal to women: "At 91 Mrs. Alvira Carter Feels it is Her Duty to Vote Republican Ticket." According to the article, Mrs. Carter (who was pictured in a photo), would be voting for the first time in her life in November's election. Making her way ("unassisted" by her daughter) into a barbershop that served as a polling place, Mrs. Carter had announced that she wanted to register as a Republican. Still possessed of excellent hearing and an adept knitter and cook, Mrs. Carter, originally from Vermont, took "a deep interest in public affairs." Mrs. Carter was quoted as saying, "I believe in voting for the best man regardless of politics."[13]

Mrs. Carter's assessment that Mayor Watt was the best man to occupy city hall came in the midst of criticism by Glynn's *Times-Union* of how Albany officials were dealing with crime. The newspaper suggested that frequent conferences between William Barnes and Commissioner of Public Safety Frost were a sign that the two were trying to come up with a plan "to stave off trouble."[14] On July 16, 1919, the newspaper reported that Albany's citizens were "puzzled" by how matters were conducted in the police department. Asserting that the police force was "inadequate to properly patrol" the growing city, the newspaper reported that Police Chief James Hyatt had said as much and been rebuked by Mayor Watt. Public safety in Albany was reported to be "controlled" by the "Big Three"—Mayor Watt, Commissioner of Public Safety Frost and Corporation Counsel Andrews. These men, the newspaper alleged, abused their power by making and breaking officers and handling departmental purchases to "suit themselves."[15]

Even as it castigated the Republican administration, the *Times-Union* declared its support of Albany police officers and their demand for a pay increase. A front-page story on September 5, 1919, announced, "Albany Police Want More Pay: Talk of Strike." City officials had been promising to consider a raise from the $1,300 per year that the officers were currently receiving to $1,500, which would bring the salaries of the force more in line with other cities. In an interview, Thomas Dolan, a veteran Albany officer and the president of the New York State Patrolmen Association, told the newspaper that the police had been asking for "fair living wages" for the past forty-seven years and each time had been "sidetracked." Although he was not completely comfortable with the Boston Police strike that was then underway, Dolan believed that the strike would make the public aware of the conditions faced by police officers in Boston and in New York State.[16]

However, the Boston Police strike went badly for the striking officers. After walking off the job, they were widely depicted as having left the city at the mercy of criminals. They attempted to negotiate as volunteers carried out their duties. Governor Calvin Coolidge proclaimed, "There is no right to strike against the public safety by anyone, anywhere, anytime."[17] When the strike ended, the striking officers were not reinstated. Having this example, Albany police officers evidently thought better of any inclination they might have had to strike. City officials also seemed ready to reach some accommodation. On September 17, 1919, the *Times-Union* reported that the Albany police had been "given new hope by Commissioner Frost."[18] On September 19, the newspaper reported that the Common Council favored more pay for the police officers.

But support for the police not withstanding, as the election approached, Glynn's newspaper continued highlighting an alleged crime wave in the city. The unsolved DeWitt Forest murder case hung over the police department's head. The twenty-six-year-old Forest had been set upon and killed after a night out with his wife and another couple. Walking home alone on Hudson Avenue, he was approached by two men and shot. Various theories of the murder included the possibility that his wife had been involved or that he was the victim of a jealous former suitor of his wife. One of the mysteries of the case was how the two men, who had lain in wait, knew that he would come along Hudson Avenue. During that month of August 1919, the details of the police investigation and shifting theories and rumors were reported in local newspapers. However, the murderers were not found.[19]

Bold attacks by robbers on innocent citizens also received attention. A *Times-Union* front-page story on October 17 recounted two such incidents side by side under the banner headline "Robbers Work Boldly; Man and Woman Held Up." The male victim lost ten dollars when he was robbed at about 6:00 a.m. by four men. He reported the crime at the Fourth Precinct, but the matter appeared to have "been suppressed" by the police. The newspaper noted that residents of Delaware Avenue, where the crime had occurred, had been complaining of the lack of "proper police protection." A number of offenses had occurred in the area, ranging from clotheslines and gardens stripped by thieves to women-accosted by strange men. There was only one plainclothes officer to cover the entire neighborhood after midnight. The other robbery victim was a "girl nurse." Returning, in uniform, from a call between 8:00 and 9:00 p.m. the night before, she had been waylaid by "footpads." The men demanded the bag she was carrying. She explained that it contained only medical supplies and begged them not to take her equipment. After looking inside the bag, the would-be robbers threw it back at her. The reporter noted that it was a shame that this young nurse, who cared for "the poorest classes of the foreign element," should not be safe as she went about her duties.[20]

Attacks on young women in their own homes received similar coverage by the newspaper. Several stories appeared about gangs of young men who loitered on city streets and harassed young women coming out of the theatre or walking home. Although well-dressed, these men were said to be without visible means of support. On at least three occasions reported by the *Times-Union*, men forced their way into the rooms of young women. These newspaper articles made no mention of rape, but the women were said to have been terrorized. These attacks occurred in the area covered by the Second Precinct, specifically Hudson Avenue and South Pearl Street. Judge Brady, the police court magistrate, was reported to be outraged by these incidents. Citizens were said to have responded with "a wave of indignation." When a suspected member of the gang was arrested, he was described as dressed in the "height of fashion" and displaying "an air of bravado." He said that he knew influential people and would soon be free. By the time he appeared in police court, he was said to be less sure of himself.[21]

By October 2, the *Times-Union* had asserted that criminals described Albany as "a harvest town." According to the newspaper, it had reached the point that any citizen who ventured out at night with money in his pocket "does so at his peril." Police blotters were alleged to "have been filled up with reports of hold-ups, robberies, second-story jobs, etc., etc." During this crisis, there was "nary a peep" from the mayor or the Commissioner of

Public Safety. Following its usual practice, the newspaper praised the Albany police officers who were the "best ever" but understaffed. However, the article included an account of another robbery, in which a young woman had been handcuffed and gagged in her own apartment and the police were unaware of what had happened until several hours later.[22]

This crime coverage and commentary by the *Times-Union* did not go unanswered by the *Albany Evening Journal*. In its pages, the *Evening Journal* sought to downplay and discredit stories of Republican neglect and incompetence in handling the crime wave that was allegedly plaguing Albany. One strategy used by the *Evening Journal* in its coverage was to report the occurrence of a crime but emphasize the victim's defeat of the offender. For example, on February 14, 1919, the newspaper reported that the trio of intruders who had tried to hold up a garage had not been able to give Henry Campbell, the night watchman, "anything to worry about." The observant Campbell had noticed that the blue touring car the men were driving when they arrived at the Rob Circle Garage on North Allen Street had no license plate. When the occupants asked for gas and then tried to rob him, he was already alert for trouble. Campbell fought the three men off with a hammer and a wrench.[23]

About a month later, the *Evening Journal* reported that a young woman also had succeeded in thwarting a crime. The young woman was an employee at Albany Perforated Wrapping Company. After parting from her companions, she continued toward home. On Van Rensselaer Avenue, near Wolfert Roost Country Club and "within 300 feet of her home," the young woman had been attacked by a man who stepped from the bushes and stopped her with questions about the people who lived on the street. As she started to walk away, he grabbed her by the neck from behind. Although thrown to the ground, the young woman managed to resist her attacker's efforts to stuff a handkerchief in her mouth. The man struck her in the face with his foot and tried to drag her away, but she grabbed a barbed-wire fence, secured a "death grip on the wire and kept on struggling." Fearing that the young woman's cries would attract attention, the man fled. He ran past the companions with whom his intended victim had been walking. They assumed that he was running to catch the trolley car. Although he escaped, the police were reported to "have a line on a young man they suspect." The young woman, who had offered such vigorous resistance to her attacker, was described as the daughter of an ice dealer, "a girl of medium build."[24]

On another occasion, the *Albany Evening Journal* chided another local newspaper for attempting to gain political capital from unfortunate events. On January 31, 1919, the *Evening Journal* objected to "hasty criticism" of the

Albany police department, which had been "unduly shrieked in a morning newspaper."[25] According to the *Evening Journal*, Police Chief Hyatt stood by his men, "who tackled three important cases" in succession. In one of those cases, a serious mistake had been made when the parents of a dead boy had not been notified. When the Third Precinct had three major cases break at the same time, a miscommunication apparently occurred between Captain Dugan and his lieutenant. No one had notified the parents of the fourteen-year-old boy that he had been the victim of a "shooting tragedy near the Wolfert's Roost Country Club." He had been killed by an eighteen-year-old friend. Neither boy's parents knew what had occurred until they became concerned that the boys were missing. The *Evening News* said that the police were "human" and that the lack of notification had been "purely accidental." However, this was another example of what Democratic critics saw as wrong with police administration in Albany.[26]

During the months leading up to the November election, the two rival newspapers highlighted the appearances by political candidates from their respective parties. These appearances before various civic groups, including those sponsored by female voters, gave the candidates an opportunity to make or respond to accusations about city government. In what reads like a retort to the charge by the *Times-Union* that the citizens of Albany were "puzzled" by how the city government functioned, the *Evening Journal* commented on a talk by Arthur Andrews, the corporation counsel. This October 1, 1919 editorial, titled "Dignified, Lucid, True," summarized the talk Andrews gave at a meeting of the City Club. The newspaper noted that Andrews's Democratic contender, William E. Fitzsimmons, "had come to deliver" a campaign speech, "and he delivered it." Andrews, on the other hand, had said that was not what he was going to do. Instead, he described for the audience "the form of government under which city affairs are administered." After he had explained the duties of the various departments, he turned to the matter of salaries for city employees. Although the *Evening Journal* does not bother to mention this, clearly Andrews was tackling an issue raised by the *Times-Union*—Albany's underpaid police officers and firemen. Andrews told his audience that the city's police officers, teachers and firemen ought to have pay increases. But, he explained, it was impossible to do that given the restriction on taxation at "two percent of assessed value of real estate." The editorial noted that the full text of the speech by Andrews could be found elsewhere in the newspaper.[27]

In editorials on October 4, the *Evening Journal* praised Mayor Watt's ten years of experience as a manager of municipal affairs. Responding to criticism about the lack of civic improvements, one editorial pointed out that the war had consumed many of the city's resources and caused delays of projects. Those projects would now be resumed with the return of peace. In another editorial, appearing beneath the previous one, the newspaper labeled as "Futile Slander" the story in the *Times-Union* (not mentioned by name) that had referred to Albany as a "harvest town" for thieves. The editorial asserted that the "political enemies of the city government have resumed their old-time practice" of making this false accusation. They were doing this in an attempt to "repair their broken political fortunes." This would not succeed because everyone in Albany "knows those who would besmirch" the city and "nobody pays attention to them."[28]

Challenging this assertion that no one was paying attention, the *Times-Union* predicted that the Barnes machine would go down in defeat. A front-page story on November 4, 1919, proclaimed, "Captain Townsend Albright Next Mayor."[29] The newspaper's prediction was wrong. Townsend was defeated by Watt. The Democrats won only one municipal office. Putting a brave face on the Democratic loss, the *Times-Union* reported that the race for mayor had been closer than it had ever been. Watt had retained his office with a margin of only 1,546 votes compared to the 10,324 margin of two years earlier.[30] For its part, the *Evening Journal* reported that Paddy McCabe's men had tried unsuccessfully to intimidate voters. In spite of the Democrats' "campaign of vilification," the city remained "safely Republican." Commenting on the slender margin of Mayor Watt's victory, the *Evening Journal* observed in an editorial that, rather than a comment about Watt, this was a "discredit to those who did not vote for him."[31]

What the election of 1919 had done was set the stage for the demise of the Barnes Republican machine. The only victory for the Democrats had been won by Daniel P. O'Connell, a young man of working-class Irish background who had campaigned in his navy uniform. O'Connell had been elected county assessor. Two years later, in 1921, Democrat William S. Hackett (1922–26) would defeat William Van Rensselaer, the Republican candidate for mayor. With that, Democrats would take control of city government. With his victory in 1919, Dan O'Connell had supplanted Paddy McCabe as the leader of the Democrat Party in Albany and began to establish his own powerful machine. As for Barnes, a few years later, in 1924, he sold his newspaper to an heir of the Singer sewing machine fortune, Stephen Clark of Cooperstown (who also owned the Albany *Knickerbocker Press*).[32] Barnes then left Albany.

But in 1919, these changes, which would sweep one political machine out of power and another in, were only beginning to manifest themselves. What was much more obvious was that the Prohibition movement had gained unexpected ground during the war years. Like the rest of the country, Albany was about to go "dry."

THE TRIUMPH OF PROHIBITION

In 1914, after agitating for a ban against alcohol in Massachusetts, William Anderson, head of the Anti-Saloon League, decided to move his base of operations from Boston to New York City. As he explained, New York City was a symbol of "wet" America to other Americans and to the rest of the world. The city was a gritty metropolis peopled by immigrants who embraced saloon culture. If the Anti-Saloon League could reform New York City and bring the rest of the state into the "dry" column, this would provide momentum for broader expansion of the movement. With Anderson's move of the prohibition war to New York, the League gained political clout as a lobbying group more quickly than anyone (including Anderson himself) would have predicted. Making skillful use of "pressure politics," the League coerced reluctant New York Republican legislators to support the organization's prohibition agenda or risk losing the next election.[33]

By 1919, if Anderson had not convinced New Yorkers of the evils of alcohol consumption, his organization and allies, such as the Woman's Christian Temperance Union (WCTU), had managed to gain public attention. The movement's campaign had forged a rhetorical link between alcoholism and other social problems. The League's successful lobbying of politicians across the country and the acceptance of the movement's goals by both ordinary citizens and millionaires such as John D. Rockefeller had set the stage for legislative action.[34] This action came at the federal level with the Eighteenth Amendment to the United States Constitution. This amendment banning the manufacture, distribution and sale of alcoholic beverages was implemented with the passage of the Volstead Act.

In Albany, citizens did not put out the welcome mat for Prohibition. A nineteenth-century temperance movement had been based in Albany. Even then, the city had a reputation for being "cool" toward the reform movement. Historically, as a Dutch settlement, Albany had been known for its taverns. Later, under British rule, Albany had been a way station for settlers headed west, providing all of the necessities, including liquor. The breweries of Albany had supplied the settlements on the frontier.[35] Now, in 1919, as Prohibition loomed, Albanians seemed more prone to join the resistance offered by the "wets" than to become "teetotalers."

When Alfred ("Al") Smith was inaugurated as governor, he supported the movement to rescind New York's ratification of the Eighteenth Amendment. Drinkers in New York and elsewhere hoped that even if the amendment stood, the statute could be modified to allow the manufacture and consumption of beer and light wines. Some supporters of the Prohibition

West of the Capitol. Note the sign on the side of the café advertising Beverwyck Lager. *Courtesy of Albany Public Library.*

amendment had assumed that beer and wine would not be included in the ban on alcohol. Members of the labor movement adopted the slogan "No Beer, No Work." They arrived in Albany displaying banners and buttons and demanding that the Legislature take up the issue.[36]

Albany Police Chief James L. Hyatt expressed his concern about the impact of Prohibition on another type of crime. Interviewed by the *Times-Union* in January 1919, Hyatt predicted that the ban on alcohol would mean that former drinkers would turn to drugs. He foresaw an increase in drug addiction. Another unnamed official, formerly involved in "the liquor branch of the government service," predicted that moonshining would increase in Albany, the rural areas of New York and throughout the country.[37]

With no other choice but to adapt or close down, breweries in Albany began to retool to make nonalcoholic beverages and other products. A January 1919 survey by the *Times-Union* found that the Beverwyck Brewing Company and several of its competitors, including the Citizens' Brewing Company and Dobler Brewery, intended to produce sodas and "near beer" (a beverage that fell within the less than half of 1 percent alcohol requirement of the Volstead Act). Beverwyck Brewing was gearing up to produce high-quality malt vinegar made from barley malt that would be marketed in Canada and Great Britain. The soda department at Beverwyck

Brewing would focus on making a "very high grade" of ginger ale, along with lemon beverages, birch beer and sarsaparilla. The reporter found that the Hedrick Brewing Company, owned in part by the O'Connell brothers, hoped to have a new beverage on the market within a ten-day period. Made from apples and barley malt, it was "declared to be a very palatable drink." Hedrick Brewing also intended to continue to make the near beer and birch beer that it had been producing for several months.[38]

Saloons and other establishments that had made much of their income from liquor sales contemplated a future in which this activity would be illegal. Shifting to the sale of coffee, sodas and other nonalcoholic beverages was one option. Closing down was another. The third was to continue to sell liquor but to try to evade detection by the "dry enforcement" officers who were already arriving in the city.

The struggle between wet and dry forces in Albany (as in the rest of the country) would continue from 1919 to 1933, when Prohibition ended. A troubling aspect of the Prohibition movement was the blatant bigotry expressed by William Anderson of the Anti-Saloon League and others in the movement toward Germans, Jews, Italians and other immigrants who had arrived in the United States in the early twentieth century.[39]

IMMIGRANTS, RADICALS, RACE AND LABOR

In 1919, in the aftermath of World War I, immigrants from Eastern Europe were often viewed as questionable material for assimilation into the "American tapestry." They were sometimes suspected of being dangerous radicals who threatened the political system. The Russian Revolution and a series of bombings in the United States that had been linked to the "radical" movement produced the "Red Scare" of 1919. United States Attorney General A. Mitchell Palmer orchestrated a series of raids aimed at rounding up socialists, communists and anarchists. In Albany, the clashes between "Reds" and law enforcement officers would come later.

In 1919, "red" also was used to describe the color of the blood being spilled in the race riots that erupted. During that "Red Summer," whites and blacks clashed as boundaries were threatened. Black migrants leaving the South were "pulled" by the hope for more social and economic opportunities. They were "pushed" by the inequalities and injustices they were leaving behind. The migration of African Americans to urban centers in the Northeast and Midwest gained momentum during and after World War I. The early twentieth century witnessed the birth of the modern ghetto in cities such as

Chicago, New York and Philadelphia. Racial tensions sometimes erupted in public spaces—such as a Chicago beach—and along the boundary lines that separated African Americans from their white European-American neighbors.

Albanians were aware of the racial violence occurring elsewhere. Albany newspapers carried wire service accounts of the race riots that occurred in Chicago and other cities. The racial divide that separated racial/ethnic groups in Albany and in the rest of the country was reflected in the language used. Newspapers identified "Negro" victims, suspects and offenders by race. This use of racial/ethnic identifiers also occurred when the person being discussed was "Chinese" or, occasionally, "Italian." By 1919, the Irish in Albany had moved into the mainstream and no longer suffered the kind of blatant stereotyping that had occurred in the nineteenth century when they were the newest immigrant group.

The labor movement was an arena in which issues of race/ethnicity, class, gender and reform crusades such as Prohibition and child labor were played out. During World War I, organized labor had experienced significant benefits in the form of "union recognition, shorter hours, higher wages, and federal mediation." As the war ended, government contracts were canceled, and millions of veterans returned looking for jobs in a declining labor market. Labor fought to hold onto the gains it had made as unemployment increased and a postwar depression began. During 1919, "more than four million workers went on strike" as both Congress and the courts became less sympathetic to labor's demands.[40]

Because Albany is the state capital of New York, labor groups organized demonstrations in the city to capture the attention of the governor and Legislature. Strikes occurred in local industries as workers responded to inflation and the need for better working conditions. In March 1919, several "textile girls" appeared before Judge Brady, the police court magistrate. Judge Brady cautioned the nearly fifty young women, who were strikers from Fuki and Hatch Mills, not to interfere with nonstrikers. This lecture was delivered to the young women (who were not under arrest) in the juvenile courtroom.[41] A strike also loomed against the United Traction Company (UTC) unless matters could be resolved by arbitration. On August 7, the *Times-Union* reported that a vote would be taken by the West Albany workmen who had been at a "fever heat of anxiety since the Chicago strike started."[42] But the strike that was to bring the violence of labor conflict to Albany did not come until 1921. As with other matters, the events of 1919 simply set the stage.

The year 1919 was a pivotal one, both in Albany and the rest of the country—the prelude to the Roaring Twenties.

Chapter 2

THE ROARING TWENTIES

If one were asked to describe the 1920s, images from F. Scott Fitzgerald's "jazz age" novel *The Great Gatsby* (1925) might come to mind. Jay Gatsby, the millionaire with the mysterious past, knows a gangster named Meyer Rothstein, who fixed the World Series (a character inspired by real-life New York City gangster Arnold Rothstein). Gatsby, who served in World War I, throws lavish parties at his Long Island mansion. Gatsby's guests, flappers with bobbed hair and young men in tuxedoes, dance the Charleston and guzzle champagne and bootleg gin. Jay Gatsby, a tragic hero, longs for the beautiful Daisy Buchanan, his lost love. Bored and constantly in search of amusement, Daisy Buchanan and her wealthy husband, Tom, drift from America to Europe and back again. They are amoral. In Fitzgerald's vision of the 1920s, Gatsby's glittering American dream comes to a violent end. In real life, it was the Wall Street Crash of 1929 that brought many dreams to an end. In those few days in late October, the economic bubble burst and the stock market tumbled.

The 1920s offered a study in contrast. The modern world was haunted by old hatreds and fears. The Ku Klux Klan (KKK), a vigilante group that had been born in the South in the days following the Civil War, had a rebirth in the 1920s. This time the organization was national in scope. Its targets included not only African Americans, but also Jews, Roman Catholics, foreigners and others who did not share the Klan's brand of "American" values. Strong in Indiana and other parts of the Midwest, the Klan was also on the rise in upstate and western New York. In 1923, Senator John Hastings (Democrat-Brooklyn) and Assemblyman James Kiernan (Democrat–Kings County) sponsored a bill that would require secret orders to register the names of their members with the state. The political process took an unexpected turn when Hastings narrowly escaped being framed for possession of drugs.

A box was left in a room that Hastings had been occupying at the Ten Eyck, a popular Albany hotel. Accompanying the box was a wallet with Hastings's initials and his personal card. The day before the delivery, Hastings had gone out of town. Taken ill, he had stayed away for two weeks. During that time, the police chiefs in Albany and neighboring Troy received letters claiming that Hastings had assaulted a young woman in his hotel room and that he had drugs in the room. When Hastings returned to the hotel, a clerk gave him the wallet, which Hastings said was not his. The wallet contained the claim check for the box, which the hotel had stored until he returned. Hastings requested that the hotel detective open the box. It contained about $500 worth of narcotics.[43] Certain that this was a plot to frame and discredit him, Hastings first suspected the Ku Klux Klan. But after three men were arrested, the frame-up was linked to a business matter. Hastings was involved in a civil suit about the disposal of stock in a mining corporation through a company in which he had an interest.

Although the KKK had not been involved in the "drug plot" against Hastings, when state legislators in Albany were "deluged" with letters, the Klan was viewed as the most likely suspect. These letters attacked Jews and Catholics and made boasting references to burning churches. Governor Al Smith, a Roman Catholic, received a letter that accused him of being "a pawn in the 'Jesuit' game."[44] In spite of these attempts to influence the legislators and the governor, the bill was enacted. It was quickly found to be ineffective when the Klan discovered a loophole in the language of the law. By incorporating, the Klan could avoid the requirement that it name its members. It did so. Then, in another twist, Justice Pierce of Buffalo, the magistrate who signed the Klan's incorporation papers, discovered that the documents had later been altered. Facing a challenge to its charter by New York Attorney General Carl Sherman, the Klan missed the filing date to request a jury trial to resolve the matter. Directing its anger at Governor Smith, the Klan threatened to lead an anti-Smith movement at the Democratic convention the following year. Smith's supporters were not concerned. The New York State KKK lacked much of the political clout of the Klan in the South.[45]

The Klan was attempting to extend its reach during an era in which both the federal government and the general public had come to believe that immigrants from Eastern Europe might be dangerous "anarchists." In 1927, the controversial case of Nicola Sacco and Bartolomeo Vanzetti, Italian immigrants who were tried and convicted of armed robbery and the murder of two payroll clerks in Massachusetts, generated heated debate.

The Roaring Twenties

An international movement formed to save the two men, who had been sentenced to death. The guilt of the two men and the fairness of the criminal justice process was challenged. In Albany, concerned about possible violence as their August 1927 execution approached, the Chief of Police placed guards on the Capitol Building and at the home of the mayor.[46]

Suppression of immigration during and after World War I created more employment opportunities for some Americans. Internal migration increased. African Americans from the South and whites from Appalachia left home to seek jobs in industries such as the auto factories of Detroit. Auto manufacturer Henry Ford (known for his anti-Semitism) offered his workers the unheard-of salary of five dollars for an eight-hour day. Men lined up by the thousands for jobs on his assembly lines, where they could make good money but were required to do mind-numbing work. Technology and efficiency worked for industries but changed the nature of work.

Even as modern technology was embraced by industry, science as it related to human evolution crashed head-on with religion. In 1925, in a courtroom in Tennessee, evolution was put on trial. High school teacher John Scopes stood accused of teaching the subject in his classroom. He was represented by famed defense attorney Clarence Darrow. On the other side, William Jennings Bryan, former secretary of state, peace advocate and opponent of Darwinian theory, presented the case for the prosecution. During what came to be known as the Scopes Monkey Trial, Bryan talked about the Bible and faith. A year earlier, during the 1924 Chicago murder trial of his clients Nathan Leopold and Richard Loeb, Clarence Darrow had evoked a new form of secular religion when he hired alienists (psychiatrists) to examine his brilliant and wealthy young clients. They were accused of the "thrill killing" of fourteen-year-old Bobby Franks. Leopold and Loeb had planned to commit the "perfect crime." Instead, they found their "aberrant personalities" being discussed in a courtroom as Darrow fought to save their lives.[47]

Alienists, influenced by the work of Sigmund Freud, also had been called to testify in the New York City murder trial of Ruth Snyder and Henry Judd Gray for the murder of Snyder's husband. The Snyder-Gray case offered a titillating mix of sex and violence to readers of respectable newspapers, as well as pulp fiction and detective magazines of the era. In an America that was increasingly focused on consumption—"buy now and pay later"—Snyder was portrayed by the media and the prosecution as a symbol of female avarice. A "brassy," stylishly dressed blonde, she failed to convince the jury or the public that she had been a devoted mother and a psychologically abused wife.[48]

The gangsters of the 1920s also engaged in conspicuous consumption. In real life, they dressed well, dined well and drove fast cars. In the films of the

1920s, to the distress of the censors, they did the same things on the movie screen. Sound would come later, at the end of the decade. But from the dawn of the film industry, Western outlaws and urban felons thrilled moviegoers. Although slower to embrace the uniformed police officers, audiences were also fascinated with the "detective"; they had been since Arthur Conan Doyle's Sherlock Holmes made his print debut in Victorian London.[49] Now, in the 1920s, there was the possibility that the detective could apply modern science to crime fighting. During the nineteenth century, pseudosciences such as phrenology (which involved the study of the bumps on a subject's head to determine character) had been popular among both crime experts and the general public. But it was fingerprinting, also invented in the nineteenth century, that survived as a legitimate crime-solving tool. A criminal could now be identified by his (or her) unique fingerprint patterns, which could be kept on file by law enforcement agencies.

Green Street between Beaver and Hudson Avenue. Note the Gospel Mission sign in the upper window and the sign for a practitioner of phrenology in the basement window. *Courtesy of Albany Public Library.*

The Roaring Twenties

The application of better methods of classifying and identifying criminals was one factor in achieving more efficient law enforcement. Police administrators such as August Vollmer in Berkeley, California, also advocated increased education and training for police officers. Founded in 1909, the Bureau of Investigation would become the famed Federal Bureau of Investigation (FBI). By the 1920s, the Bureau was already viewed as the premier law enforcement agency in the United States. The Bureau was led by a young and ambitious director, J. Edgar Hoover, who promoted his agency to the media. With the rise of the Bureau and the creation of "the public enemies" list by the Chicago Crime Commission, American mythmaking about ruthless gangsters and crime-busting G-men (government men) was off to a heady start.[50]

NEW YORK'S "GRAY RIDERS"

At the state and local level, law enforcement was also evolving. In 1917, the bill that would create the New York State Police passed by one vote. Governor Charles Whitman signed the contested bill "over the objections of trade unionists, farmers, and Civil Service reformers."[51] The next year, the Democrats in the Legislature, none of whom had voted for the new agency, attempted to abolish it. Distrust of a state police force ran deep. A similar proposal had been defeated in New Jersey. Only one other state—Pennsylvania—had such a law enforcement agency. The New York State Police was modeled on the Pennsylvania State troopers. The two wealthy women who had championed the idea of a state police force in Pennsylvania envisioned it as an agency that could provide protection for rural residents. But the Pennsylvania State Police was also sent into the coal fields of Pennsylvania to intervene in the strikes by miners and used in steel and transit strikes. The agency had gained the reputation of "Black Cossacks" on horseback employed on the side of the industrialists. During the four-year campaign for state police in New York, advocates downplayed the image of state police officers as strikebreakers. Instead, they focused on crime fighting, particularly in rural areas.[52]

The first commander of the New York State Police, Superintendent George F. Chandler, was a physician and National Guard officer. He drew on this background as he developed a model for the new police agency. During the next four months, Chandler consulted officials of the Canadian Mounted Police and Pennsylvania State Police.[53] He also consulted with writer Katherine Maynard and her associate, heiress M. Moyca Newell. These

Two mounted troopers searching the Model-T Ford of a suspected bootlegger. Note the beverage cases on the running board. *Courtesy of the New York State Police.*

two women were the driving force behind the creation of the Pennsylvania State troopers. Later, Chandler named the first state police training camp "Newayo" in their honor.[54]

In addition to qualifications, which included superior physical fitness and the manners of a gentleman, Chandler determined that each recruit must also be an experienced horseman. As a mounted patrol stationed in barracks across the state, the troopers were to be sent out in pairs to rural areas. Concerned that his men have the right look, Chandler designed a "distinctive gray cloth uniform set off with a purple tie and purple band in a Stetson hat."[55] The citizens who saw them on horseback gave the troopers the nickname "the Gray Riders" for the color of their uniforms. This was certainly more preferable than "Cossacks." However, by 1919, the state police had been deployed during a steel strike, and officers were criticized by labor for the tactics used. One of the early tests of the New York State Police came in 1921, when the trolley car workers employed by the United Traction Company (UTC) went on strike in five upstate cities. Albany was one of those cities.

THE TROLLEY STRIKE OF 1921

Lasting ten months, the streetcar strike of 1921 was "one of the longest mass transit strikes in American history"[56] This strike marked the end of two decades of confrontations between UTC and Division 148 of the Amalgamated Association of Streetcar Workers (AASREA). The first successful strike against the company by the workers occurred in 1901. The streetcar workers went on strike again in 1910, when the company initiated a transfer policy. That policy pitted North Albany streetcar workers against those in nearby Cohoes and seemed aimed at weakening the union. In 1915, the Albany streetcar men supported a strike that had been initiated by the streetcar workers in neighboring Troy. Believing in industrial democracy, the streetcar workers insisted on "the rights of representation, participation, free speech, and due process in the workplace."[57] Made up predominantly of Irishmen who also shared ethnic ties, Division 148 was an exceptionally strong union.

During World War I, cost cutting led streetcar companies across the country to replace two-man cars with one-man cars. This was the threat local streetcar workers faced. They also were concerned about the firings that had occurred as the United Traction Company "asserted itself aggressively in discipline matters."[58] The strike of 1921 came about, in part, because of the refusal by United Traction to negotiate with the leaders of the union. The company had announced that it would have to roll back the salaries of motormen and conductors from an hourly wage of sixty cents to forty-five cents. The streetcar workers already were being paid sixty cents after having successfully negotiated a raise. The company argued that the salary increases had been based on the expected approval of a fare increase by the Public Service Commission. The commission had denied the company the requested ten-cent fare increase. Albany fares increased to eight cents and those in Troy to six cents. Bypassing the union, UTC sent the workers a memo informing them that salaries would return to the hourly wage of forty-five cents that had been in place on June 30, 1920. Although the union was willing to engage in arbitration, the company rejected that option. This was seen by the workers as an attempt by the company to weaken the union by refusing to negotiate with its representatives.[59]

In an editorial on January 27, 1931, the *Times-Union* urged the two sides to try to make "[e]very effort" to avert a strike. The paper argued that a strike in "the dead of winter would be a calamity" for the communities served by the streetcar system. The paper also argued that the streetcar system was "a public utility" even though it was privately owned. The streetcars used public streets with public permission. But by January 31, the newspaper had concluded that both sides in the conflict had decided "the public be damned." In this editorial, the newspaper reminded Albanians of what had happened during the strike of 1901, when there had been mobs, street fights and bloodshed.[60] Meanwhile, believing the strike was inevitable, Albany Police Chief James Hyatt began to put a plan into place. In late January, he warned his officers that they should be prepared for a long strike.[61] Knowing that Albanians who chose not to cross the picket line would seek alternative transportation, Hyatt attempted to set fifteen cents as the maximum price that could be charged by jitney (an unlicensed taxi or small bus) drivers.[62] On February 3, 1921, the *Knickerbocker Press* reported, "Fifty Policemen Ordered to Guard Street Car Barns."[63] One of the problems for Hyatt was that strike duty would stretch his force to the limit. For State Police Superintendent Chandler, the strike in Albany would provide an opportunity to prove that the New York state troopers could function effectively in a large city.

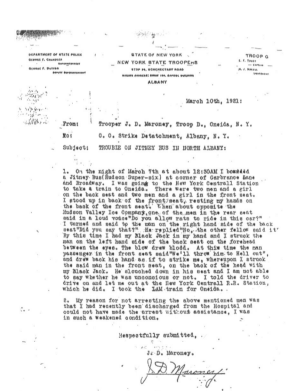

Memo from a state trooper about an incident on a jitney bus in North Albany, March 10, 1921. *Courtesy of the New York State Police.*

The Roaring Twenties

At 6:00 a.m. on January 29, 1921, the strike began. The "all-night" crews returned their streetcars to the "barns" where they were kept. Then they walked off the job. Over thirteen hundred workers in Albany and Troy were now on strike. Three other neighboring cities—Cohoes, Watervliet and Rensselaer—were involved in the strike.[64] Despite efforts by civic and business leaders to bring the two sides to the negotiating table, no settlement could be reached. The *Times-Union* expressed concern about the "dangerous" presence of strikebreakers who would be pitted against the streetcar workers.[65] With UTC guards protecting the car barns at Quail Street and North Albany, mounted police officers escorted the streetcars. The streetcars now were being operated by four hundred professional strikebreakers who had been brought in by UTC to keep the streetcars running.[66]

Strikers and strike sympathizers launched attacks against the streetcars. Overhead electric wires were cut. Passing streetcars were pelted with bottles, snowballs, bricks and other items. After three days of riots, public transportation was brought to a standstill. On February 9, 1921, two hundred state troopers were sent to Albany to restore order.[67]

During a Lincoln Day speech, Republican leader William Barnes denounced the strike, referring to labor as "a commodity." His political foe,

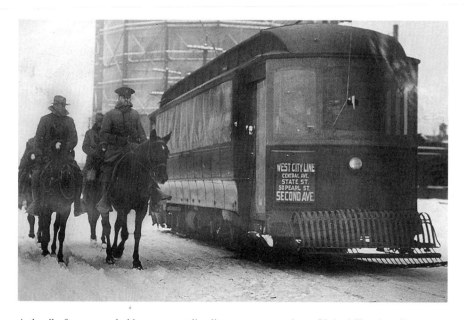

A detail of troopers, led by a state police lieutenant, escorting a United Traction Company trolley car during the Albany Transit Strike, February 1921. *Courtesy of the New York State Police.*

Martin Glynn, responded in an editorial in the *Times-Union* that supported the strikers and scolded Barnes for his use of the word "commodity."[68] Among Albanians, support for the strikers was strong. "We Walk" clubs were formed, and boycott petitions were signed by "tens of thousands" of citizens. On March 14, the *Evening Journal* reported that H.B.Weatherwax, vice-president of the United Traction Company, had complained that the strikers were using intimidation to keep citizens from riding the trolley cars.[69] Later that month, arguing that the jitneys were illegal, he asked Mayor Watt and the officials in the other four striking cites to stop the jitneys from providing service.[70]

On March 6, 1921, Chief Hyatt was quoted as "acknowledging a crime wave in Albany." However, Hyatt linked this crime wave—holdups, robberies and thefts—directly to the strike. He said that it was common to have crime go up in cities where strikes were occurring. Criminals followed strikebreakers into town because they knew that the police would be too busy keeping peace and order during the strike to focus on their regular police duties.[71] A few days later, both peace and order in Albany were disrupted when an explosion, suspected to be the work of strikers, shattered windowpanes of houses in North Albany. The explosion appeared to have been caused by several "railroad torpedoes tied into a bunch and placed on the track." The target of the explosion was the "strikebreaker special," on its way back to the North Albany barn.

The explosion occurred between Wilson Street and Livingston Avenue near Broadway. The streetcar was partly wrecked. Nine houses nearby suffered damage to glass in doors and windows. The two New York state troopers who were escorting the car on a motorcycle with sidecar were flung to the sidewalk. An automobile carrying a "flying squadron" of Albany police officers was thrown against the curb on the other side of the street. Two men were injured. The state police arrested a core maker who was standing in the doorway of a nearby saloon. He was charged with disturbing the peace and held without bail. The saloon in front of which he had been lounging was shut down by order of Captain Dugan of the Third Precinct.[72] By now, there was enough concern about strike-related crime that the regular session of the grand jury was extended in order to "deal with the traction situation."[73] That month, the Albany police department began its eighth week of strike duty. The *Knickerbocker Press* reported that the force of fewer than two hundred men was now working fourteen- to eighteen-hour days.[74]

United Traction continued to take a hard line toward the strike.[75] UTC argued that the union leaders were not employed by the company, had not been for several years and were therefore not empowered under the existing

Broadway #751 (near Livingston Avenue), in the Arbor Hill area. Note the "For Rent" sign in the window. *Courtesy of Albany Public Library.*

contract to engage in arbitration. In court, the union suffered a series of defeats, including an injunction from conspiring "in any manner to interfere with" United Traction business operations. Strikers and strike sympathizers were forbidden from congregating and picketing.[76] But some Albany police officers sympathized with the strikers—"thirty-two members of the police department had formerly been platform men for the UTC."[77] Sympathetic Albany police officers "harassed" strikebreakers ("scabs") and directed citizens in need of transportation toward jitneys rather than streetcars.[78]

In May 1921, a strike sympathizer shot a streetcar conductor. Later that same month, someone threw a brick. It struck a passenger who was on his way home aboard the Pine Hills trolley. The passenger's skull was fractured. After lingering for almost two weeks, he died.[79] On May 20, the *Knickerbocker Press* reported, "Business Zone Swept By Worst Strike Riot; 1,000 Storm Trolleys."[80] A day later, the *New York Times* reported, "Albany Rioters Stone Street Cars and Fight Police."[81] That same day, state troopers charged a crowd at Union Station after a man was shot in the leg.[82]

Instead of calling in the militia, state, city and county officials agreed to leave, restoring order to Chandler's state police officers. By May 22, 250 state troopers were en route to Albany. The United Traction Company had stopped all night operations.[83] On May 24, the *Times-Union* reported,

"State Police Patrol Streets in Helmets, Armed with Rifles." That day, the state police was on patrol in downtown Albany, ordering those who had gathered to move on. Later, there were complaints that some troopers had used their clubs on people in the crowd. One case that was reported involved the manager of the postal telegraph and his son. Wire operations were down for an hour after the incident. An investigation was pending.[84]

The question was whether the state troopers could bring order to the city or if the National Guard would have to be called in. Chandler argued that his men could handle the job. When the strike began, he had declared, "We can stay until hell freezes over."[85] Chandler argued that his state troopers could remain in Albany on duty longer than the National Guard and do the job with fewer men. By May 25, 1921, Albany officials had concluded that he was right and the National Guard would not be needed.[86]

Although union members in the Albany and Troy locals voted to continue the strike, by July they were facing financial problems. They received support from other locals of AASREA to keep them going. But by the end of July and into August, individual strikers began to approach the company about returning to work. By the time Democrat William Hackett was elected mayor in the November 1921 election, the strike was moving toward a close. The union had been crushed. It was forced to agree to the conditions set by United Traction. The company would use one-man cars; strikers were required to apply for their old jobs in order of seniority; and, although the streetcar workers might maintain their union membership to keep their insurance, the union could no longer negotiate for the workers.[87]

Even though UTC had survived the strike and set the terms for settlement, the company, which had been concerned about increased postwar operating costs, continued to lose money. By 1928, it had been sold.[88] Streetcars in Albany, as in other cities, would soon become outmoded, replaced by buses, taxis and private automobiles.

But that would come later. In 1921, after a resolution had been negotiated between United Traction and its employees, streetcar service returned to normal. Both the state police and the Albany police force returned to other duties. In his annual report to the Commissioner of Public Safety, Albany Police Chief Hyatt observed:

> *The past year proved to be a very busy one in police circles. The members of the department were called upon to do extraordinary work during the long strike of the employes [sic] of the United Traction Company, and they are to be commended for the able and efficient manner in which they conducted themselves during the trying and serious conditions which prevailed.*[89]

The driver of the city bus waits for his passengers, circa 1930, while a man patiently smokes his pipe. *Courtesy of Albany County Hall of Records.*

Hyatt added that although they had been required to render "constant and continual service" and had no opportunity to see their families "for weeks at a time," the men did not complain and "were ever ready both day and night, to render the services they were required to perform."[90] For both the Albany Police Department and the state troopers, the lengthy strike had been a test of their abilities and dedication to the job.

During the rest of the decade and into the 1930s, Prohibition-era crimes offered another challenge to city and state law enforcement officers. One aspect of that challenge was how they would work with federal law enforcement agents.

Going "Dry"

The first Prohibition raid of an Albany saloon by federal agents was reported on February 6, 1920. A squad of "Revenue men" entered Maxwell's saloon/café on Broadway. They searched the establishment and took away what was presumed to be alcohol for analysis. The proprietor, John J. Maxwell, agreed to make a voluntary appearance that afternoon for an interview with the agents. News of the raid caused "great excitement in saloon circles" because

Maxwell's was a prominent establishment "patronized by some of the best known men about town." The raid had been conducted without fanfare. The patrons who were present at the time had not been ordered to leave. Still, the raid was taken as "proof that the government means business."[91]

If Prohibition enforcement had worked as its supporters expected, law-abiding citizens would have given the federal government's "dry" agents full support and cooperation. Instead, many otherwise law-abiding citizens violated the Volstead Act. This meant that the enforcement tasks assigned to the "dry" agents were more difficult than had been anticipated by the Anti-Saloon League and its allies. A fundamental problem from the beginning was that there were not enough agents to do the job they had been assigned—to prevent the manufacture, distribution and sale of alcohol in the entire country. The Anti-Saloon League had insisted that these agents not be a part of the civil service system. The League believed that keeping the hiring process outside the civil service system would give prohibitionists more political control and ensure that only men who were dedicated to the Prohibition cause would be hired. What actually happened was that the men who were hired often had no law enforcement experience, gained the job through political connections and might have limited commitment to the law they were assigned to enforce. The environment in which they functioned placed the underpaid dry agents at constant risk of being offered bribes not to do a difficult job.

By 1920, the Albany police department had begun some Prohibition enforcement. The *Argus*, a local newspaper, reported on October 21, "Two Held After Police Raid Nets Big Liquor Stock." The raid was conducted by officers from the First Precinct who raided a garage on Warren Street. They found a truck and a touring car loaded with one hundred cases of whiskey. The whiskey was turned over to the "dry" agent in charge of the Albany office. According to the newspaper, this was the most important strike "against illegal trafficking in liquor since the citywide raids of last spring." The police suspected that an Albany "ring" might be in operation.[92]

Police officers in New York State would soon have a clear mandate to enforce Prohibition law. On April 5, 1921, Republican Governor Nathan Miller signed the Mullan-Gage Enforcement Law. This law created a state-level equivalent of the federal Volstead Act.[93] State, county and municipal police officers in New York were charged with carrying out enforcement of the federal Prohibition Act. The law was unpopular because of its strictness and because of the burden it placed not only on New York law enforcement agencies, but also on courts required to provide jury trials for defendants arrested under this law. By 1923, Senate Democrats, with the aid of four

The Roaring Twenties

Republicans, were able to pass the Dunnigan bill, which repealed the Mullan-Gage law.[94] Thereafter, New York police officers had no statutory obligation to aid in the enforcement of federal Prohibition laws.

In 1923, Reverend Wallace Marsh, the district superintendent of the Anti-Saloon League, presented Mayor Hackett with a report about the vice activities that a League investigation had uncovered in Albany. According to Marsh, many of the houses of ill repute (brothels) that the League found were "within a stone's throw of police headquarters." Marsh and the League asserted that Albany was wide open to bootleggers and women of the street. The mayor reportedly assured Reverend Marsh that if he would provide information about these activities, the police would take action. A sworn statement from the Anti-Saloon League provided the location of the houses of prostitution at addresses on Division Street and the saloons operating on Broadway, Beaver, Sheridan and Central Avenue.[95]

From a practical standpoint, municipal, county and state police agencies had a number of reasons to continue to participate in the enforcement of some aspects of Prohibition even after the Mullan-Gage law was repealed. As a matter of efficient law enforcement, the state police shared the federal dry agents' interest in intercepting large shipments of liquor being transported by car or truck. Because the troopers were involved in routine enforcement of traffic laws on the highways of upstate New York, they sometimes stopped vehicles for offenses such as speeding and discovered contraband liquor in the vehicle. In Albany, arrests for public intoxication rose significantly when Prohibition went into effect. Intoxicated citizens caused problems when left to their own devices. They were sometimes profane, abusive and/or dangerous to themselves and others. And in Albany, as in other cities during the era, the fines that could be levied against these offenders were a boon to the city's revenue.

But the numbers seem to reflect the level of enforcement as much as actual offending. In the first two years of Prohibition (1920 and 1921), intoxication arrests actually dropped (1,037 in 1919; 477 in 1920; 660 in 1921). Arrests then began an erratic climb to 1,456 in 1922, 3,555 in 1923 and an all-time high of 4,118 intoxication arrests in 1924. Arrests fell to 3,635 the next year and, thereafter, remained between 2,100 and 3,000 until the end of Prohibition.[96]

Along with its focus on intoxication arrests, the Albany Police Department had to deal with the presence of adulterated and sometimes deadly liquor, sold on the black market to unsuspecting Albanians. Prohibition had created a black market for both liquor from legitimate manufacturers and the "moonshine" and "bathtub gin" produced by entrepreneurs. When substances such as lye and industrial alcohol were added to increase the quantity and add color or "a kick," the product could be toxic enough to send the consumer to the hospital or the morgue. As early as 1919, the presence of "poison" alcohol in Albany was reported. On October 31, 1920, the *Argus* reported that two men had been found dead in an old building after drinking poison alcohol.[97] The men were identified by papers found on their bodies. Both men were from New Jersey. On May 28, 1921, the *Times-Union* reported that a man had been "blinded and crazed by Prohibition whiskey."[98] A similar headline appeared in the *Albany Evening Journal* on May 27, 1922.[99] He was the second victim in Albany in two weeks. The next day, on May 28, the *Knickerbocker Press* reported that "poison whiskey" was being made in two hundred places in Albany. Officials were said to be "nearly helpless under present law" to stop this activity. The article included a warning to readers from doctors not to drink any "colored concoctions."[100]

In June 1920, a "poor man's club" was being established in Albany in a renovated building on Hudson Avenue. This "club" was described as the "first attempt to find a substitute for the saloon since the start of Prohibition." The superintendent was to be W.A. Merrill, the founder of the Broadway Gospel Mission. An "excellent colored chef" had been hired to oversee the preparation of the food that would be served in the cafeteria at cost. A man who had no money could work for his meal. The club would offer other amenities, including smoking rooms. Those in attendance at a planning meeting included ministers and representatives from the Anti-Saloon League, the Albany City Mission and the Salvation Army.[101] Such alternatives to saloon culture were also appearing in other cities.

However, based on the reports of raids and arrests, a significant number of Albanians disregarded Prohibition. Albany was "wet." Liquor could be purchased in saloons, hotels and other establishments that were no longer supposed to be selling alcohol. It was available as well in the illicit "speakeasies" that sprung up after Prohibition began. Raids of these Albany speakeasies were frequent occurrences during the 1920s. One series of raids, conducted over forty-eight hours in January 1929, received coverage in the *New York Times*. During these two days, seventy federal agents from out of town came to Albany on a "flying visit." During that month, since New Year's Eve, 135 raids had been conducted in Albany. All of this activity came as Agent Canfield, the new "dry" chief, declared his determination that Albany would be "at least 85 per cent drier than it has been for some time."[102]

In 1926, New York legislators had enacted "the Baumes laws." Named for Caleb H. Baumes, chairman of the New York State Crime Committee, these laws included a forerunner of the modern "three strikes and you're out" law. Under the Baumes laws, fourth-time offenders received mandatory life prison terms. Whether this deterred Prohibition-era crime was open to question and continued to be debated into the 1930s. Critics of the legislation, including Governor Franklin D. Roosevelt and Warden Lewis E. Lawes of Sing Sing Prison, argued that the people being sent to prison for life were often petty offenders, rather than the violent, felony offenders that the legislation intended to deter.

In the case of the Prohibition rumrunners and bootleggers, the opportunity for fast and significant profits from their investments made the illegal manufacture and distribution of liquor worth the risk. The money to be made drew men who lived in the Adirondack towns near the United States–Canadian border into the business of "rumrunning." Many of these rumrunners were not professional criminals. They were men who found that driving a car for a bootlegger or going into business for themselves earned them more money than they could make in rural upstate New York by other means. Even upstate farmers got into the business by providing a barn where the rumrunner could hide his car and his shipment. The irony of this was that prior to Prohibition, there had been more support for the dry option in this region than could be found downstate. Now, these upstate towns and cities were seen as outlaw towns where many of the residents were either involved in rumrunning or supportive of criminal friends and relatives. The hostility between upstate, border communities and the government increased when dry agents started firing on the vehicles of rumrunners while in pursuit.[103]

Although Canada also experimented with prohibition during this era, in the province of Quebec the manufacture and sale of alcohol was legal. Prohibition in the United States proved an economic boon for Quebec as tourists from the United States crossed into Canada to party. These tourists sometimes attempted to smuggle a flask, bottle or case of liquor back across the border. As the United States Customs Agency became more aware of the ingenious ploys used by the tourists, more liquor was intercepted. However, the rumrunners who purchased large amounts of liquor and brought it back into the United States used fast cars and backcountry farm roads to evade customs agents, dry agents and the state police.[104]

The route for the rumrunners ran from Canada to New York City. Albany was the midpoint on that route. Some shipments found their way into markets in Albany and surrounding towns and cities. Local newspapers carried occasional reports of shipments of beer or alcohol that had been intercepted in the Albany area. A truck also might be intercepted, not by law enforcement officers, but by hijackers.

Albany newspapers routinely reported the actual or alleged corruption of dry agents or police officers. These stories came from across New York and the country. At the local level, there were occasional incidents, such as the dry agent who was arrested for accepting bribes from liquor dealers. On another occasion, an Albany police officer and an unidentified woman were stopped near Elizabethtown in the Adirondacks. They were found to have a case of what appeared to be Canadian ale in the car.[105]

Even as law enforcement officers kept an eye out for rumrunners who were bringing in alcohol, they were aware that the route between New York City and the Canadian border was also attractive to drug dealers. In 1914, the Harrison Narcotic Tax Act was enacted by the federal government. This early legislation was aimed at both domestic drug consumption and the international traffic in opium. In the early twentieth century, rhetoric about drugs reflected two overlapping concerns: (1) the reputed relationship between drug use and crime by members of racial minority groups and (2) the feared seduction of susceptible white men and women into drug use. The Harrison Act placed a special tax on the production, importation, sale and distribution of opium and coca leaves. In 1924, the importation of heroin into the United States was banned. Federal agents were assigned to enforce the federal narcotic laws. New York's state narcotics laws were enforced by state and local police officers.

DRUG PEDDLERS AND OTHER "UNDESIRABLES"

A stereotype of the 1920s linked specific racial minority groups with certain drugs: the Chinese with opium, Mexicans with marijuana and African Americans with heroin. In 1924, a local newspaper reported that an "Albany Chinaman," who was a member of a tong (a secret society or fraternal organization), had sought approval for a gun permit from Police Chief Frank Lasch. The man was said to be a member of either the Hip Sing Tong or the On Leong Tong and to have been afraid of violence because of a tong murder in Schenectady, a neighboring city.[106] Another article made mention of concern on the part of "Albany's Chinese" after murders in New York City and Hartford, Connecticut, that "tong warfare would spread to Albany." The Hartford victim was said to have been a "big gambler" with investments in "several Albany banks."[107] However, there is no indication that the feared violence actually did materialize.

What seems true is that Albany drug dealers were a diverse group. For example, in August 1931, the *Evening News* provided an account of a series of raids carried out by narcotic agents with the assistance of the Albany police. These raids were said to have "struck a severe blow" against opium trafficking in Albany. Five men and two women (apparently the wives of two of the men) were arrested. The raids had occurred after an investigation by federal agents, some of them from New York City. Among the suspects arrested was a doorman at the Kenmore Hotel. His employer said that the doorman had been dismissed from his job. Taking the opportunity to protect his hotel's reputation, the manager also added that gangster "Legs" Diamond had never stayed at the hotel under his own name and Diamond had been ejected after the publicity from his trial in Troy (see chapter 3). As for the doorman, Hamilton, he was identified in the newspaper account as a "Negro." So were two other suspects. Not identified by race, the two couples had the surnames "Flynn" and "Nardolello," respectively.[108]

On the advent of Prohibition, Albany Police Chief Hyatt had predicted that the ban on liquor would cause former drinkers to turn to drugs. There is no indication in the annual police reports that arrests for drug offenses went up significantly following the start of Prohibition. As with intoxication arrests, the number of arrests for state narcotic law offenses actually went down. In 1919, thirty-one people were arrested, but in 1920, the number was only eleven and in 1922, only six. As with the intoxication arrests, the state narcotics law arrests surged in 1922, when twenty-five arrests were made, and again in 1923, when the number was up to twenty-seven arrests. The following year, the number dropped back to sixteen.[109]

Throughout the 1920s, federal agents conducted drug raids in Albany. In March 1922, six Albany drug dealers were sent to the federal prison in Atlanta under the escort of a federal marshal, deputy and three guards from Utica.[110] In March of the following year, the chief federal narcotics agent in Albany praised the local force for its help in carrying out a series of raids in the "tenderloin" (red-light district) that had resulted in arrests and the seizure of $50,000 worth of drugs.[111]

Newspaper reports indicate that the "drug peddlers" operated out of private homes, as well as speakeasies, poolrooms and other locations frequented by their potential customers. Drug law enforcement was a part of the larger "crusade" against vice in Albany that reform groups demanded and Albany officials said was being conducted.

In December 1920, Police Chief Hyatt ordered his men to start a "round-up" for the investigation of all "undesirables" with "shady reputations." According to the *Argus*, Hyatt ordered his men to "take extra measures" to protect the city's shopping district. He also approved the assignment of mounted patrols in the Pine Hills neighborhood, where residents had asked for additional police protection.[112] Crime was seen as a threat to both the business district and neighborhoods. The drug dealers and their customers were among those "undesirables" who were seen as a significant part of the crime problem.

On September 20, 1921, officers from the Second Precinct raided a poolroom at 56 Division Street for the fourth time. Four men were taken into custody, and 147 "decks" of cocaine and morphine were found. The suspects were taken before the U.S. commissioner and then committed to jail to await trial. The poolroom at 56 Division Street was said to be the gathering place for men who hung out on the corner from morning to night.[113] Only two days later, on September 22, Albany police carried out a fifth raid on the poolroom at the same location.

In an interview with the *Knickerbocker News*, Captain Dugan, commander of the Second Precinct, said that his plainclothes men went frequently to the poolroom and it was kept under surveillance. He explained that it was difficult to get evidence against the criminals who gathered there. The reporter observed that it had "been impossible to find out from the police" who owned the Division Street poolroom. Federal agents had been involved in making arrests there the night before.[114] Several robberies in the business section of Green and adjacent streets had been attributed to the poolroom patrons.[115] The area around Green and Division Streets was described by the newspaper as a "popular hangout for the criminal elements." Businessmen in that vicinity also expressed the need for more "police supervision" of the "dope district" at State and Green Streets.

In January 1922, a new commander, Captain "Sam" Kirth, took over the Second Precinct. He announced a "cleanup" of the precinct, ordering a crackdown on all "undesirables, from panhandlers to gamblers." The first to be arrested in this sweep were the "loafers" at Union Station. A few days after taking charge, Kirth conducted an "inspection tour" of his precinct that was reported to have attracted "big crowds" of onlookers.[116] Several months later, in March 1922, Police Chief Frank Lasch initiated a night patrol. The patrol was aimed at the "bandits and other 'bad' men" remaining at large. Chief Lasch hoped that the police would be able to make arrests in the murders, holdups and burglaries that remained unsolved.[117]

In an interview with the *Times-Union* in February 1928, Police Chief David Smurl called drugs "the greatest menace that exists in the country today." However, he said, the cooperation between the Albany police and federal agents had put Albany "in better shape as far as the drug situation" was concerned than most other cities. According to Chief Smurl, drug trafficking was "funny" in that it tended to "run in streaks." In Albany, the trafficking was mainly in opium. The chief offered his thanks to the Hearst newspapers (of which the *Times-Union* was one) for their "continuing drive" against drug trafficking.[118]

The annual reports by the chiefs of police during the 1920s and local newspaper coverage indicate that "vice" crimes in Albany ran the gamut from disorderly houses and prostitution to the drug dealing discussed here. But in Albany in the 1920s, gambling was a bigger political "hot potato" than other forms of vice.

GAMBLING AND POLITICS

In January 1921, the *Knickerbocker Press* reported that the police department was on a "gambling crusade" and was "clamping a lid" on poolrooms. These "alleged horserooms" were forced to close their doors.[119] However, Police Chief Hyatt allowed other, presumably legitimate poolrooms to stay open on Sunday "despite state law" to permit bowlers to use the facilities. He did, however, enforce the closing law against hotels, not allowing them to have Sunday dancing.[120] Later that same year, the police department engaged in a "new drive" to abolish the "giant ball pools" in Albany. In August, six suspects were arrested as the result of an investigation by a private detective. The detective had been employed by District Attorney Timothy E. Roland. Working undercover, the detective had purchased lottery tickets from the suspects.[121]

Arrests continued over the next two years, but gambling in Albany was tenacious. In April 1923, Mayor Hackett (who heard from a number of reform groups that year) received a letter from the New York State Civic League. The Civic League informed Hackett that gambling was still "rife" in the city in spite of Hackett's promise to clean it up.[122] Throughout the 1920s, as during the era of William Barnes's Republican machine, there were repeated assertions from various groups and individuals that gambling was widespread in the capital city. In 1923, Albany police officers made twenty-three arrests for keeping slot machines. This was up from seven the year before. Arrests remained high compared to previous years, with nineteen arrests in 1924 and twenty-one arrests in 1925.[123] The fact that slot machines, lotteries and other forms of gambling continued to flourish under both Republican and Democratic administrations suggests that gambling in Albany was both deeply rooted in and protected by the political machine that happened to be in power.

Although the local newspapers reported police efforts to break up crap games or drive out illegal slot machine owners, the "baseball pool" was paramount in the debate about discretionary law enforcement in Albany. This lottery had begun as low-key wagering by employees of the J.B. Lyon Printing Company during the era of William Barnes's Republican machine. When the pool began to attract attention from outsiders, the company lottery was shut down. The baseball pool continued as a private operation by an employee. By the 1920s, the pool had become a large-scale gambling syndicate that operated in New York, Massachusetts and several other states.

During the 1920s, Republican politicians complained that, under Democratic governors, gambling in Albany was allowed to go unchecked, while it was suppressed in those counties where Republicans were dominant. In 1920, his political foes cried foul when Democratic Governor Al Smith announced an assault on corruption and gambling in Republican-controlled Saratoga. According to the *New York Times*, Smith was responding to a complaint that a member of the Saratoga Chamber of Commerce had made to George Chandler, the commander of the New York State Police. The chamber member was said to have expressed concern about the return of gambling houses to Saratoga. Before leaving for the Democratic National Convention in San Francisco, Smith was reported to have sent a letter to the sheriff of Saratoga County and the mayor, giving them notice that "gambling houses must not be tolerated" in the city. In his letter, Smith emphasized the sizable investment of taxpayer money in preserving Saratoga Springs as a "health resort," with spas that could rival those of Europe. Smith threatened to relieve both Saratoga officials of their duties and have state troopers police the city if the gambling houses were allowed to return.[124] In 1926, he carried through with his threat by removing the Saratoga officials.[125]

As for gambling in Albany, his political enemies alleged that the baseball pool was operated by Dan O'Connell, head of the Albany Democratic machine, and his associates. In 1920, John ("Solly") O'Connell, brother of Dan O'Connell, was arrested on a gambling charge. On September 9, 1921, the *Times-Union* reported, "3 More Taken As Agents For Gambling Pool." In 1925, Governor Smith instructed the sheriffs of Albany, Schenectady and Rensselaer Counties to put an end to the baseball pool. On May 3, 1925, Claude C. Tibbitts, the Albany County sheriff, said that the Albany baseball pool had been broken after numerous raids and arrests. Sheriff Tibbitts said that gambling was no longer widespread in Albany County, but he would continue his investigation.[126]

The next year, in December 1926, a federal grand jury was investigating the Albany baseball pool (also operating as the "Hudson Pool" and the "Clearing House Pool"). According to investigators, the prizes ran "as high as $7,000," and "staggering sums" of money were being wagered each week on "baseball statistics, clearing house quotations and other figures." In New York and New England, those involved allegedly included "politicians, bookmakers, barroom keepers and race track agents." The investigation had begun when a bank clerk in Boston who pled guilty to embezzlement said that he had lost more than $10,000 playing the pool. Eight suspects were said to be ready to turn state's evidence.[127] The next day, December 4, 1926, thirty-six people were indicted. Six of them were from Albany.[128]

An August 1927 statement by the Republican State Committee accused "prominent Democrats" in Albany of having "profited largely" through the baseball pool. The Republican Committee placed the blame for gambling and bootlegging in Albany on the Democrats. The statement referred to the "cleanup" that had been prompted by the "leadership of a ministerial association" that was opposed to public gambling. The protests by this reform group had caused the Democratic politicians holding "high office at Albany" to engage in "at least cursory police activity." Aside from the revelations about gambling that had been confirmed by the indictments handed down by the federal grand jury in Albany, investigations had also revealed a "well-organized and apparently unrestricted red-light district."

This reference to an unrestricted red-light district recalls the allegations in the Democratic-led "Albany Inquiry" during the era of the Barnes Republican machine. In its 1927 statement, the Republican Committee noted that the new "padlock law" was being used in the legal procedures against "keepers of these dens of vice." This law allowed such establishments to be closed and padlocked for one year. The Republican statement asserted that the end result of this "housecleaning" in Albany would be to return to "good government under Republican administrators."[129]

In October 1927, a couple of months after the Republican Committee issued its statement, the *Albany Evening News* reported that Police Chief Smurl had ordered an "Albany vice cleanup." After hearing complaints about disorderly houses operating in Albany, Smurl said that he intended "to get to the bottom of the matter." He denied that his action was prompted by any "specific report" or by "the declaration of Colonel Theodore Roosevelt [the son of the president]" that "vice is rampant in Albany." Smurl went on to state that he was uncertain that vice did exist in the city, but if it did, "I am going to see that it is broken up." Smurl ordered a twenty-four-hour police detail in those sections of the city where vice had flourished in the past. Police officers were instructed to make arrests at "first indication" of law violations related to Prohibition, gambling or disorderly conduct.[130]

Lieutenant Colonel Theodore Roosevelt continued to press the charge he had made about gambling in Albany. In a statement made public by the Republican State Committee in November 1927, Roosevelt alleged that Governor Smith was politically indebted to New York City's Democratic machine, Tammany Hall. Because of his dependence on machine politics,

Smith was failing to see that gambling laws were enforced in the state Capitol. As proof of what was going on in Albany, Roosevelt pointed to the indictment of Daniel O'Connell and his brother, John, by the federal government. He criticized Governor Smith for accepting the statements from the Albany County sheriff and the District Attorney that gambling pools had been shut down in Albany. Roosevelt argued that Smith could not fail to know that gambling was going on in Albany. It was common knowledge. Or Smith could have asked his own lieutenant governor, Edwin Corning (a political ally of the O'Connells), to inform him about what was happening.[131]

Whatever the state of gambling in Albany, Governor Smith continued to express concern about gambling in Saratoga Springs. The following year, in November 1928, the *New York Times* reported that plainclothes state troopers had been sent into that city to investigate gambling and vice. This came after the July 1928 sentencing of three Albany men to eight months each in prison for their involvement in the Albany baseball pool. One of the men, who had been a mail carrier for twenty-four years, lost his job and his pension. He was fined $750. He had a wife and eight children. The other two men, clerks in Albany stores, were fined $500 each. The defense attorney in the case asked for mercy, arguing that the pool had been conducted "absolutely on the level" with no "fixing." The Albany baseball pool was now said to be out of business because of the federal prosecutions.[132]

However, the next month, United States Attorney Cool reported that evidence from recent raids in Albany and Troy indicated that pools were "thriving." It was estimated that $50 million passed through the various pools in New York and nearby states.[133]

In September 1928, Clarence Barnes, the Republican candidate for New York State attorney general, attacked Governor Smith. Barnes alleged that the Hotel Ten Eyck in Albany was the "headquarters" for the pool, which Smith allowed to continue to do business. Barnes claimed that on June 4, "men higher up" had met at the hotel to divide $100,000. William Pringle, alleged treasurer of the Albany pool, was under indictment in federal court.[134] That same month, en route to the Republican Convention, Lieutenant Colonel Theodore Roosevelt stopped in Albany to testify before the Albany grand jury about the pool. While in the city, he had breakfast at Hotel Ten Eyck.[135]

In February 1928, the *Times-Union* had reported that the wife of William Pringle, the alleged baseball pool treasurer, said that Bill "won't squeal." She was said to be seeking aid from Daniel O'Connell. By August 1929, O'Connell himself was facing a federal grand jury. He had been called in the perjury trial of James J. Otto. Otto was already serving time in the federal prison in Atlanta on a perjury charge related to the baseball pool. O'Connell had been fined $500 in Boston after pleading guilty to aiding in the operation of the pool. He had been arrested at his camp (summer home) in the Heldeberg Mountains, west of Albany, by a deputy marshal. O'Connell's lawyer argued that O'Connell had been arrested illegally. A New York City judge overruled the objection to the warrant and fixed O'Connell's bail as a material witness at $10,000.[136]

However, O'Connell refused to answer questions posed to him during his grand jury appearance on the grounds "that to answer might tend to incriminate and degrade him." Brought before the judge, he was directed to answer the questions he was being asked.[137] On December 18, 1929, O'Connell failed to appear in federal court in New York City to plead to an indictment charging him with perjury. A bench warrant was issued. Four other Albany witnesses appeared in the New York City in answer to subpoenas and bench warrants.[138] The absent O'Connell was reported to be in Canada with plans to go to Havana, Cuba. His bail of $10,000 had been forfeited.[139]

On January 7, 1930, Attorney James Cuff, who was representing O'Connell, denied that his client was a fugitive. He said that O'Connell had "no more intention of running away" than did the prosecutor.[140] A day later, O'Connell surrendered in Albany. His bail was set at $30,000. Three months later, in April 1930, a federal appeals court ruled that O'Connell must serve three months for contempt of court.[141] On June 14, 1930, the *New York Times* reported, "O'Connell is Jailed in Ball Pool Case." In the "compromise agreement," O'Connell was to serve ninety days in federal prison. The agreement provided for dismissal by Federal Attorney Tuttle of action on the perjury indictment. In exchange, O'Connell withdrew his continued appeal of the contempt sentence and began serving time. He had gone to prison the day before.[142] But this was not the last to be heard of the pool in Albany. In June 1931, a year later, Governor Franklin D. Roosevelt announced his determination that the pool in Albany and Rensselaer "be stopped at once." He was reported to have written to the sheriffs in the two counties and to the chiefs of police.[143]

Gambling in Albany, the capital city of New York, proved to be both a chronic crime problem and a chronic political issue. It could be used to call into question the commitment of political opponents to root out corruption and enforce the law or to argue that political alliances determined how the law was enforced and where. But although the controversy about law enforcement in Albany focused on gambling and other vice-related offenses, year after year, the largest number of arrests by the Albany police were for traffic law violations.

CARS, DRIVERS AND THE LAW

On March 29, 1922, a new crime-fighting plan by Albany Commissioner of Public Safety Keith and Police Chief Lasch was announced in the *Albany Evening Journal*: "Armed Cars to Patrol Streets of Albany to Curb Crime." Police officers equipped with revolvers and rifles were to patrol at night in their vehicles. They were to arrest the owners of automobiles who sat in parked cars with their lights off or drove their cars without lights.[144] The next day, the *Knickerbocker Press* reported that the night patrol to fight crime in Albany would include "motorcycle and auto squads" that would "scour all sections of [the] city to avert law violations." The newspaper noted that this recalled "trooper activities during trolley strikes."[145]

During the Prohibition era, the automobile moved to center stage in the war between "cops" and "crooks." For example, the Volstead Act allowed the confiscation of vehicles that had been used to transport alcohol. But first the cops had to catch the crooks. The newspapers provided accounts in the slang of the day of criminals who sped away from a crime scene in their "get away cars." The newspapers also reported on the violent ends of gangsters who had been "taken for a ride" or were found in their "bullet-riddled" cars. With criminals in cars, police officers were reassigned from walking their beats to patrolling in cars. As police historians have noted, this move into vehicles enhanced police response time but isolated police officers from citizens.

There was another issue related to the car. That was the increase in routine law enforcement duties as more automobiles appeared on city streets and state highways. In 1923, Mayor Hackett kept his promise to add more police officers to the Albany force. The police department had lost a number of officers, including two captains who were dismissed or allowed to retire when they were found to be physically unfit according to the standards set by the state constabulary. Hackett had announced his intention to remove police officers and firemen who had gotten their jobs not because of their physical ability to do the work but because of political appointments. But his decision to hire thirty additional police officers was also a response to the increasing pressure on the department to enforce parking and traffic laws.[146]

By the 1920s, Americans from all walks of life had fallen in love with the automobile. Advertisements in magazines and newspapers invited them to experience the mobility, freedom, convenience, status and/or luxury of owning the latest model. Moreover, advocates argued that the automobile would bring city and rural areas closer, making it easier to move between the two (to live in the country and commute to the city to work or shop). Those who were concerned about the rapidly increasing

Lynn Block, Grand and Beaver Streets. The Albany public market. Albanians also gathered here to listen to the World Series. *Courtesy of Albany Public Library.*

number of automobiles pointed out that these vehicles were also sources of urban congestion. In cities, both in the North and South, drivers had already begun the now common process of searching for some place to park. Merchants of downtown stores worried that frustrated drivers would simply give up and go away. Available parking in most cities was far from catching up with the demand.

The impact of the car on American culture was being discussed by auto club members, politicians, civic leaders, businessmen and the general public. As car ownership increased and more drivers took to the road, the number of car accidents rose. Across the country, traffic safety became a matter of concern. For example, the *New York Times* reported in June 1921 that De Forest J. Mobie, a magistrate in Schenectady who had been struck by an automobile, was waging a campaign to "curb speeders" on a notoriously dangerous four-mile section of the Albany–Schenectady Road. Ignoring the thirty-miles-per-hour speed limit, speeders had been responsible for sixty-one accidents, ten deaths and at least twenty-one injuries the year before. Officials noted that this state road was popular with bootleggers making their runs back from the Canadian border.[147]

In Albany, as in other cities, police officers directed traffic. In July 1924, Mayor Hackett removed a number of officers from traffic duty at

Two children wait for the policeman's sign to cross the street safely after leaving Public School 21 on 666 Clinton Avenue in 1931. *Courtesy of Albany County Hall of Records.*

intersections after the installation of automated signals. But even with the use of new technology such as traffic lights, some issues related to cars and drivers required leadership by the state. In 1924, the first New York Commissioner of Motor Vehicles, Charles A. Harnett, was appointed. He immediately began a campaign to improve safety on the streets and highways. As part of this process, he began suspending the licenses of drivers who had violated traffic laws. Lists of drivers whose licenses had been revoked and their offenses were released at regular intervals and published in newspapers. The public exposure of these drivers indicated the seriousness with which traffic offenses were being viewed. Until 1934, New York State drivers who committed minor traffic offenses were charged with misdemeanors and instantly acquired a criminal record. This was changed that year when the Legislature decriminalized minor violations, reducing them from misdemeanors to traffic infractions.

Concern continued about the more serious traffic offenses that resulted in injury or death. One issue in vehicular homicides was how the offending driver should be charged (with manslaughter or some other offense?). In Albany, the annual report from the Chief of Police to the Commissioner of Public Safety included a brief description of each traffic accident that resulted in a death. For example, according to the 1934 report, eighteen people "met their death in auto accidents." Among these fatalities were five children under the age of twelve. The account of the death of a seven-year-old boy who lived on Elizabeth Street notes that he was "struck by an automobile on Second avenue [sic] near Grand View Terrace. Died at Albany Hospital from injuries received."[148]

The annual police report also included comments about death by other means. Although less frequent than accidental vehicular homicides, murder both intrigued and disturbed Albanians.

MURDER IN ALBANY

Street brawls and fights between men, and occasionally women, were not unusual. Murders, especially those among intimates, were rare enough to receive intense coverage by local newspapers. Throughout the 1920s and 1930s, Albany averaged about three murders per year, with only one in 1920, 1922, 1934 and 1935, and highs of five in 1926 and six in 1930, 1931 and 1933.[149]

Occasionally, a murder in Albany played into the "jazz age" journalism of the era as a tale of illicit sex and violence. On September 3, 1921, the *Albany Evening Journal* covered the story of Mrs. Rose Forrest, age twenty-four. Mrs. Forrest, known as "Broadway Rose," left her husband and became mixed up with a "bad gang." She lived with a man named Nick Nassara for three weeks. Mrs. Forrest was "shot by her lover when she decided to rejoin her husband." According to witnesses, Nassara shot Mrs. Forrest on Division Street, shortly after 8:30 a.m. Although the crime had occurred "in full view of several men," none of them had attempted to stop Nassara as he fled down Green Street and around the corner.[150]

But perhaps Albanians were more disturbed by the case of Albert Devine, the ex-alderman and Republican ward leader who killed his wife. On December 5, 1925, the *Times-Union* reported that Catherine Devine had been "murdered in cold blood by her husband." The newspaper reported that the body had been exhumed that afternoon. Devine, who was employed as a draftsman in the West Albany shops and was "highly respected," had killed his wife on September 8. Then he had buried her body under the front stoop of their house at 764 Central Avenue.

Devine's arrest came after his son, who was staying with his paternal grandmother in Philadelphia, told the police about a conversation with his father. When he was in Albany on September 12, he had asked his father where his mother was. Devine confided to his son that he had killed her. The boy went back to his grandmother's house but was unable to keep the secret. He told his grandmother, who took him to the Pennsylvania State Police. A trooper brought the boy to Albany to tell his story to the Albany police. Devine was arrested and, after intense questioning, confessed to the murder of his wife. He said they had been quarreling while on a trip to Bennington, Vermont. The quarrel continued when they arrived home. His wife accused him of talking to other women. He accused her of drinking too much. He picked up a hammer and "struck her on the head with it." After carrying her body down to the cellar, he went out through the cellar window. He dug a hole and buried her under the porch.

To exhume the body, before modern crime scene investigators, the police brought in several "gardeners." When Mrs. Devine was dug up, the damage to her body indicated that her head had been bashed in with several blows from a claw hammer. Although Devine said he had thrown the murder weapon away on Sand Creek Road, a hammer was found in a drawer in the house. As with modern cases, newspaper coverage of the Devine case included comments from neighbors. The neighbors said that they had often heard the couple quarreling, but none of them had thought the quarreling serious enough to end in murder.[151]

Briefly, it was believed that a second victim might be buried under the porch at the "Central Avenue Death House." This search for a second body was based on the statement from Devine's son, who believed his father had an accomplice. He thought that his father might have killed the man who helped him and also buried his body under the porch. The police questioned Mrs. K.G. Barnes, an employee at the Empire Decorating Company, because Devine's son had said she was involved with his father.[152] Although he pleaded not guilty to the charge, Devine's own confession helped to convict him of murdering his wife. He was sentenced to fifteen years in prison.

The next year, the *Times-Union* reported another hammer attack by a husband on his wife. Mrs. Thomas Harley, thirty-five, was found lying unconscious in her own blood. Her head had been terribly battered, and she was taken to the Albany Hospital. Her husband, Thomas Harley, thirty-three, was reported to have confessed to the crime to Assistant District Attorney John T. Delaney and Assistant Police Chief David Smurl, but no charge had yet been filed. Mrs. Harley's skull was fractured in several places. The hammer and a bread knife were found on the floor nearby. The newspaper pointed out an eerie coincidence between this case and the Devine murder. The Harleys lived at 764 Clinton Avenue. This was the same number as the Devine house at 764 Central Avenue.

A third crime involving love gone wrong was different from the other two. First, because the case involved a "tough guy" and his girlfriend. Second, because those who knew the couple thought that he might someday kill her. That day came in February 1928, when Mike "Whitey" Watts's girlfriend, Marie William, tried to leave him to return to her parents in Hartford, Connecticut. A letter from her father urging her to come home was found in her suitcase. The newspaper coverage of the case reflected the "jazz-age journalism" of the era. Earl W. Waldron, the reporter covering the story for the *Times-Union*, wrote, "Jazz and gin took its toil [*sic*] again last night." Watts had been a bartender and was known as an "Albany underworld denizen." In what Waldron described as a "sordid ending of a sordid romance," Watts slashed his girlfriend four times with a pen knife. Then he fled her rooming house at 24 Jay Street. She fell, bleeding, into the arms of one of the police officers who responded to the call. Marie was "fed up" and had been going home. Watts had responded with violence fueled by gin. He said, after slashing Marie, "I guess I fixed that girl." When he was captured, he confessed to her murder.[153]

DEATH ROW APPEALS

In the "jazz journalism" of the 1920s, tales of sex and violence were presented to a mass readership that was fascinated by the details of the lives of those involved. The Ruth Snyder–Judd Gray triangle that had led to the murder of her husband, Albert, received massive media coverage during the trial in New York City. Snyder and Gray were on death row. Their fates and those of two other death row prisoners rested in the hands of the governor of New York. Of the four who waited to see if their sentences would be commuted from death to imprisonment, Snyder and Gray were the most famous. The third was Louis Mason from Buffalo, who had been convicted of participating in the murder of David Karam. The fourth of the death row prisoners seeking a commutation was a twenty-four-year-old Albany man, Charles Doran, whose most ardent supporter and champion during his appeal was his mother.

Charles Doran and two accomplices had been accused of the murder of Raymond Jackson, a war veteran who owned a filling station on New Scotland Avenue. One of the three, Theodore Harrington, was tried and acquitted. Doran's other alleged partner in the crime, Floyd Damp, turned state's evidence. Damp made a statement in which he accused Doran of firing the fatal shot. Damp was sentenced to fifteen years in prison. Outraged by his sentence when her own son was facing death, Doran's mother stood up in court and yelled that Damp was a "squealer" and a "skunk." Although Doran had confessed to the shooting, he later declared his innocence. In the appeal of his case, his lawyer argued that the confession had been coerced by the Albany police. This accusation would later receive national attention when the Wickersham Commission (see chapter 3) made reference to the Doran case.

After suspenseful media coverage, the governor rendered his decision. He denied Doran's appeal of his death sentence. The appeals by Snyder and Gray also would be denied, as was that of Louis Mason, an African American man who had participated in a robbery that resulted in the death of a white lunch counter owner. In the case of Doran, Governor Smith "broke all precedents," according to the *New York Times*,[154] when he issued a public statement about why he had not been moved by the efforts of Doran's mother and others to save his life. Smith explained that the accused men had committed a "felony homicide." Even if it were true that Doran was innocent—as he now insisted—that did not matter. Using the opportunity to instruct the public, Smith explained that whether Doran pulled the trigger or someone else did, by his presence, Doran was guilty of murder. The law proscribed that all participants in a felony that resulted in a homicide be held accountable for that crime.

What distressed his defenders was that Doran alone faced death for the crime. His alleged partner had managed to shift the burden of the murder to Doran. However, much the same had happened in the Mason case, which also involved a felony homicide. Mason's accomplice, Julius Gibbs, was at first sentenced to death. After Gibbs testified against Mason, his sentence was commuted to imprisonment. He claimed that Mason had gunned down the victim, David Karam. As he went to his death, Mason's final words were, "Good-bye, fellows. I'm innocent." As for Charles Doran, he had nothing to say before he died in the electric chair. But he seemed to have taken to heart the advice given him by his younger brother during their final visit together. His brother told Doran to "hang tough." Doran's last words to his brother were "So long, kid. Take it easy!"

Both Doran and Louis Mason were reported to have been "in high spirits" as they each, in turn, bade the other death row prisoners goodbye as they passed their cells. Each shook hands with Judd Gray and wished him luck. Because she was a woman, Ruth Snyder was lodged elsewhere in the prison. The moment of Snyder's execution would be captured by a photographer from a tabloid newspaper who had strapped a camera to his leg. As for Doran, he would return to the headlines with the publication of the Wickersham Report, which commented on the behavior of the police in his case.

There is one other murder in Albany that should be mentioned. That one happened in the 1930s, as the end of Prohibition was approaching. That was also the decade of Albany's most famous kidnapping.

1. South Pearl Street (east side near Second Avenue) slaughterhouse. *Courtesy of Albany Public Library.*

2. A pawnshop on Hudson Avenue at the northeast corner of Green Street. *Courtesy of Albany Public Library.*

3. The ship *San Vincente* docks at the Port of Albany in 1931. The Port of Albany officially opened in June of the following year. *Courtesy of Albany County Hall of Records.*

4. First Street, looking east from North Swan Street. *Courtesy of Albany Public Library.*

5. Pearl Street (South) at the corner of Hamilton Street, 1935. *Courtesy of Albany Public Library.*

6. Spencer Street, south side, below Broadway. *Courtesy of Albany Public Library.*

7. Eagle Street below Madison Avenue. *Courtesy of Albany Public Library.*

8. The Anthony Brady Maternity Home at 30 North Main Avenue also provided medical care for infants. *Courtesy of Albany Public Library.*

9. People wait to be ferried across a riverfront street during the flood of 1936. Heavy rains and melting ice made the Hudson River overflow regularly until dams were constructed to prevent this. *Courtesy of Albany County Hall of Records.*

10. Two boys try out the new ball field by Hackett Junior High School in 1931. *Courtesy of Albany County Hall of Records.*

11. Children line up for a turn on the swings at the city playground on Cherry and Green Streets in 1937. The Floyd Reynolds warehouse can be seen in the background. *Courtesy of Albany County Hall of Records.*

12. The Temple Baptist Church stands on the corner of Clinton Avenue and Ten Broeck Street in 1937, with the steeple of St. Joseph's Roman Catholic Church visible in background. *Courtesy of Albany County Hall of Records.*

Chapter 3

A MURDER AND
A KIDNAPPING

On February 18, 1921, in the midst of the streetcar workers' strike in Albany, the *Knickerbocker Press* reported, "Gangsters Defy 'Cops.'" In a fight between the Albany police and a gang that neighbors said sounded like a riot, the police were "forced to shoot and batter their opponents with their night sticks." The fight occurred after the gang caused trouble during a dance at the Elm Club in Union Hall. The dance had an "unusually big" attendance because it was being given as a benefit for the striking streetcar workers. The first encounter began inside the hall when members of the gang and other guests at the dance got into a quarrel about a young woman. Policeman Stephen Donnelley was attending the dance as a guest. He tried to intervene in the argument. Although he was in civilian clothes, someone in the gang recognized him and shouted, "He's a cop! Grab his 'gat!'" Officer Donnelley had not drawn his "gat" (gun). He was shoved into a checkroom, where the gun was taken away from him, and was beaten about the head and face with brass knuckles. Meanwhile, several telephones calls went out to the police. Five officers arrived separately from the First, Second and Fourth Precincts. The fighting appeared to be over, and the officers emptied the hall unaware of Donnelley in the checkroom.

It was near midnight by now, and outside the officers spotted the gang members who had been involved in the argument. A fight ensued between the police and the young men. Eventually, four men were arrested. Two had been "battered with clubs." Several other suspects, one of whom might have been wounded, escaped from the scene in an automobile. Among those arrested was John Oley, an eighteen-year-old clerk who lived on Sheridan Street. This appears to have been the same John Oley who would later figure in both Albany's most famous murder and most famous kidnapping. Oley's three companions that night were from Sheridan or Orange Street. Like him, they were barely out of their teens, ages eighteen, nineteen and twenty. One was a tin smith, another a chauffeur and the third a clerk. Friends of the men sent coffee, sandwiches and cigarettes to them in jail.[155] The *Knickerbocker Press* reported that on the next day, February 19, 1921, the arraignment of the men was well attended by "politicians, little and big" who were there to "do what they could" for the men. Professional bail bondsmen were also present, but Judge Brady denied bail. The men were charged with assault, second degree.[156]

By the 1930s, the myth of the Prohibition "gangster" was complete. The "talkies"—movies with sound—allowed audiences to experience the fast-talking, tough, brutal gangster played with bravado by actors such as Paul Muni, James Cagney, Humphrey Bogart and Edward G. Robinson. These film gangsters might rise, but according to the Production Code adopted by Hollywood producers to avoid censorship by the government, "crime must not pay." By the 1930s, G-men were taking on gangsters—Al Capone in Chicago and rural gangsters such as John Dillinger, Pretty Boy Floyd and Ma Barker and her sons—in real life and in films. Although J. Edgar Hoover hoped that citizens would root for the G-men, the gangster as presented in popular culture had the same appeal as the Western outlaws in dime novels and later in films. In the midst of the Great Depression, gangsters lived well. They had style, attitude and guts.

On August 25, 1931, the *Times-Union* carried an interview with Albany Police Chief Smurl. This was the fourth in a series of interviews with prominent Albanians who had seen the gangster film *The Star Witness* that was playing at the Strand Theatre. At the end of the interview, Chief Smurl said that the film industry was in a position to educate people about "crime and its prevention." He thought *The Star Witness* was "a splendid example" of how an entertaining film could "hammer home the message that Americans and not gangsters must run this country." The earlier part of Smurl's interview was of even more interest. The police chief explained why Albany was "free of organized crime." Smurl said that his policy was to stop organized crime in its tracks by having his officers watch all points of entry into the city—"railroad, river, roads"—and bring in for questioning anyone who looked suspicious. These suspicious characters were fingerprinted, and their descriptions were sent to other law enforcement agencies. The other strategy that had proved effective, Smurl said, was the use of vehicles, or "prowl" cars, with officers armed with "the deadliest of weapons—a sawed-off shot gun." Smurl expressed his pride in his tough, honest, efficient officers, who had been instructed by him to show no mercy to criminals.[157]

A Murder and a Kidnapping

Although organized crime never gained the kind of foothold in Albany that it had in Chicago or New York City, gangsters did bring their blend of glamour and danger upstate. In New York City, Dutch Schultz and Jack "Legs" Diamond were among the gangsters who made names for themselves as Prohibition tough guys. District Attorney Thomas Dewey waged war with "the Dutchman." Legs Diamond spent a lot of time in lineups but managed to avoid conviction.

Dutch Schultz was once arrested near Albany. Legs Diamond died there.

Legs and Associates

John (Jack) "Legs" Diamond acquired his moniker because of his skill on the dance floor. Even off the floor, he was dapper. At least for a while, he also seemed to be impossible to kill. By the time he died in Albany on December 13, 1931, Legs Diamond had acquired another nickname: "the clay pigeon of gangland." Two recent attempts on his life had left him with a limp and in less than perfect health. But the two men who came to the rooming house at 67 Dove Street to kill him were so impressed by his ability to survive that they shot him three times in the head. A witness who heard what was transpiring reported that one of them said, "Oh, hell! That's enough! Come on."[158]

On the morning—about 5:30 a.m.—that he died, Jack Diamond had once again proved his ability to avoid conviction. This was a skill that he shared with Edward "Monk" Eastman (a.k.a William Delaney). By then, Eastman was long dead, but he had been an old-time gangster. Eastman had once stayed for a while in Albany after getting out of prison. In the pre-Prohibition era in New York City, Eastman led the infamous "Cherry Hill" gang (also known as the Eastman gang). The gang's archenemy was the Five Point Social Club. Eastman's gang had evolved as an organization that could provide assistance to politicians in getting out the vote and muscle for clients who needed to teach someone a lesson. In one trademark episode, Eastman and an associate, Joseph Brown, were arrested after a former coachman alleged that they had assaulted him at the behest of his former employer. The coachman had refused a command from his employer's wife to stop the coach and fetch her dog when it jumped or fell out of the vehicle. The coachman informed the lady that he had been hired to drive. He was fired for insulting her and was later allegedly beaten up by the two men. Eastman and his associate were arrested and put on trial, along with David Lamar, the Wall Street broker who had employed the coachman. Lamar said that he had hired the men to protect his wife. He denied conspiring with them and his brother-in-law to assault the coachman. Lamar said that Eastman and Brown were no longer in his employ when the coachman was attacked and provided an alibi of his own. When Lamar was acquitted by the jury, Eastman and Brown also were set free.[159]

Eastman seemed invincible until he and a partner tried to rob a drunken young man who had tottered out of a restaurant counting his money. Unfortunately for the holdup men, the young man was being followed by two Pinkerton detectives who had been hired by the young man's family to keep an eye on him. The detectives and the holdup men scuffled. Shots were exchanged, and one of the Pinkerton men was wounded. The arrival of police officers prevented Eastman and his partner from making their escape. The young man, who was said to be of a socially prominent family, had no memory of what happened and never appeared in court. Eastman was convicted of first-degree assault on the Pinkerton detective. He was sentenced to ten years in Sing Sing Prison, where he proved to be a "model prisoner." This worked in his favor when a change in New York law made all first-term prisoners eligible for parole after serving half their sentences.

After five years in prison, Monk Eastman was free. Hearing about this, the New York City police were not particularly concerned. Eastman's old gang had scattered. Eastman himself seemed to find it wiser not to go back to New York City. He is said to have lived inconspicuously in Albany for several years, before getting into trouble again by committing a robbery. With a police alert out for them, Eastman and his partner persuaded an unsuspecting chauffeur to allow them to hitch a ride down to New York City. They were arrested there. But Eastman went on to serve in the military during World War I. Just as he had been a model prisoner, he turned out to be a heroic soldier. Wounded, he escaped from the hospital and went back to join his unit at the front. His commanding officers were so impressed with Eastman that after the war they petitioned the governor of New York to give Eastman a pardon for his past offenses. The governor granted the request, and Monk Eastman assured reporters that he intended, henceforth, to be a law-abiding citizen. Eastman was killed in New York City on December 26, 1920, by Jerry Bohan, who was said to have worked as a Prohibition agent. Eastman and Bohan had been drinking together in a café. After an argument, Bohan followed Eastman to the entrance of the Fourteenth Avenue subway station and shot him.[160]

Eastman's end was not as spectacular or as memorable for Albanians as Jack Diamond's demise would be. But what Eastman and Diamond shared in common—other than having spent some time in Albany—was the ability to pursue a dangerous career for years with minimal legal consequences.

A Murder and a Kidnapping

As had Eastman, Diamond had multiple arrests but spent little time behind bars. While in the army, he served time in Leavenworth military prison for desertion. As a civilian, he had a short sentence in 1914 to the workhouse (or to Elmira Reformatory) on a burglary charge.[161] Diamond had numerous encounters with the criminal justice system. These encounters generally ended in a wisecrack from Diamond that irritated or amused the police officers who were questioning him.

Following in his brother Eddie's footsteps, Diamond got his start in organized crime working for James "Little Augie" Orgen, a New York City gangster. At age twenty-five, Little Augie was shot dead on a crowded street. According to the *New York Times* coverage of his funeral, he had been the "black sheep" son of "respectable folks."[162] Shot by Little Augie's assassins—two bullets near his heart—Jack Diamond refused to talk when the police interviewed him at Bellevue Hospital.[163] Later, Diamond was reported to have taken a job as bodyguard to Arnold Rothstein, the famous gambler. Rothstein, too, was killed. Arnold Rothstein had put up Diamond's bail a few years earlier. When Diamond was questioned about Rothstein's murder by the New York City prosecutor, District Attorney Crain, he said that it would probably be hard to find the person who had killed Rothstein because the gambler had been disliked by many people and had many enemies. Crain repeated this statement to the press and relayed that, in Diamond's "best opinion," Diamond had only conversed with Rothstein about twelve times. Rothstein was a "casual acquaintance" who had been "a frequenter" of Diamond's nightclub. Crain was reported to have found Diamond's responses "unsatisfactory."[164]

This meeting between Diamond and Crain took place on March 27, 1930. Looking back, it had been a busy month for Legs Diamond. A few days earlier, he had been in General Sessions (court) under indictment for a double murder that had occurred on July 13, 1929, in the Hotsy Totsy nightclub (of which Diamond was part owner). About a month earlier, one of Diamond's associates, Charles Entratta, had faced the same charge. Entratta had been acquitted when the prosecution had been unable to provide witnesses. Diamond's name had not come up during Entratta's trial. When Diamond appeared at General Sessions, the indictment against him was discharged. He was about to walk out of court a free man when federal agents arrived to arrest him for having jumped bail in a drug case. The forfeited $15,000 bail had been put up by Arnold Rothstein, the gambler whom Diamond claimed to know only slightly. When he was arraigned before the United States commissioner, Diamond came up with another bond, this time for $10,000. A few days later, he had his conversation with the District Attorney about Arnold Rothstein.[165]

The next month, the "bullet-ridden body" of George F. Miller from Brooklyn was found in his parked car. The car was parked in front of a building in Newark. Before it was found in New Jersey, Miller's car had often been seen at Diamond's summer home in Acra, New York (the Catskills). Miller was reputed to have been a member of Legs Diamond's gang. The police knew that he had received a $100 money order from Charles Entratta, the other suspect with Diamond in the Hotsy Totsy nightclub shooting. The detectives on the case thought Miller's murder was probably some type of gang reprisal, but they were not sure by whom.[166]

Diamond himself seemed invincible to both his enemies and the workings of the criminal justice system. On July 16, 1930, the *New York Times* reported, "Diamond in Tombs Again, May Get Out." Diamond was a suspect in another New Jersey murder and two holdups. According to the newspaper, it was his twenty-third arrest. Diamond was brought in for a lineup at police headquarters, a practice that allowed detectives to familiarize themselves with known criminals. After denying that he had been involved in the murder and two robberies in Newark, Diamond got "a roar of laughter" by giving his occupation as an automobile salesman. The police described Diamond as a "notorious gangster" who had been charged with murder five times in

A state trooper and sergeant escort the dapper "Legs" Diamond from the courthouse during his trial for the torture of a Greene County farmer. *Courtesy of the New York State Police.*

his twenty-two prior arrests.[167] Two days later, Diamond was released on the Newark charges because the witnesses couldn't identify him.[168]

On those occasions when he came upstate, Diamond often stayed at his summer home in Greene County. He also spent time around Albany for reasons that the police believed were related to his business as a bootlegger. On April 29, 1931, the *New York Times* reported, "Attack Tale Spurs Diamond Clean-Up." The tale of an alleged attack had come from the eighteen-year-old son of the Cairo, New York farmer who Legs Diamond and his gang were accused of assaulting. A couple of weeks earlier, the father, Grover Parks, had claimed that Legs Diamond and his gang had stopped him as he was driving a truck with a load of apple cider. The elder Parks claimed that he had been beaten and tortured by the gangsters, who wanted to know for whom he worked. The claim by the son that he had also been waylaid and assaulted created excitement in the community. Later, the young man retracted his statement, telling the police that it had been a hoax to get attention. Not certain whether he was lying the first time or the second, the New York attorney general ordered all of the material witnesses in the investigation detained in the county jail. Young Parks was allowed to go home.

That same day, the attorney general launched an investigation into Legs Diamond's activities in Greene County. The order for the investigation—that included a search for Diamond's brewery operations—came from Governor Roosevelt. Republicans in Greene County were suspicious of this "clean-up." But Legs Diamond himself was unaware of what was going on. Two days earlier, he had been shot by two men with pump guns while he was dining with his mistress, Marion "Kiki" Roberts, at the Aratoga Inn. The attack had left Diamond near death. A passing farmer rushed him to the Albany General Hospital in his car.

In 1930, a few weeks after he beat the charges in the Newark murder and holdups, Diamond was shot in his room at the Hotel Monticello in New York City. Two men were seen fleeing the scene. Now, Diamond had been the victim of another assassination attempt. He would survive this one, too. In May 1931, the case was still being built against Diamond by the attorney general. His records were being collected. Kiki Roberts, who had been staying at the Kenmore Hotel, had disappeared when state troopers and an Albany police detective went to pick her up for questioning. But Legs Diamond was arrested in the hospital. Attorney General John J. Bennett moved to begin the trial as soon as possible. The *New York Times* reported that Bennett hoped that he could get the two more convictions of Diamond that would allow the court to apply the Baumes fourth offender law.[169]

Before the trial began, there was an attempted break-in at the Albany hotel where Bennett and his aides were working. The authorities suspected that members of Diamond's gang were attempting to recover the papers that had been removed from Diamond's safety deposit box at the Cairo National Bank. But the prowler who entered an adjoining room where the papers were stored stumbled over a chair, alerting the two deputy attorneys general who were asleep in the next room. The prowler managed to escape, but without the papers.[170]

Three weeks after being shot at the Aratoga Inn, Diamond was well enough for plans to already be underway for his departure from the hospital. He was to be escorted by state troopers, riding behind, in front of and in the car with him. The Greene County grand jury had returned fourteen indictments against Diamond and his gang. The prosecution expected additional charges to be brought, with the trial beginning in early June.[171]

After being released from the hospital, Legs Diamond stayed at the Hotel Kenmore under police guard. On July 9, 1931, the *Albany Evening News* reported that Diamond's presence in Albany while on trial in Troy had prompted Chief of Police Smurl to assign an around-the-clock police guard to the gangster. This was intended to serve the overlapping functions of protecting Diamond and keeping out the "undesirables" who would bring their gang warfare to Albany. Earlier that week, Diamond gang member Charles Entratta had been shot and killed in New York City.[172] The next day, Diamond gave an interview to a reporter from the *Albany Evening News*. It was Diamond's thirty-sixth birthday. He admitted to the reporter that he expected the trial to be a physical ordeal because he was still partially paralyzed from his injuries. The reporter noted that, typical of members of the underworld, Diamond was accustomed to being out and about at night and sleeping during the day. But Diamond said he was "resting up mostly" and "trying to get enough strength together" for the trial.[173]

As the trial began in Troy, the case that the prosecution had constructed began to falter. The defense produced several witnesses who provided Diamond with an alibi, claiming he had been in Albany at the Hotel New Kenmore at the time when Grover Parks claimed he was beaten and tortured. The defense suggested that the slow-speaking farmer had made up the story to get publicity. The prosecution urged the jury to "have courage" and convict Diamond for his crimes. After one hour and fifty-two minutes of deliberation, the jury acquitted Diamond. However, on July 14, as the first trial ended, Diamond still faced federal charges for violation of Prohibition law.[174] Detectives were also sent to Maine to look for a former masseur at the Kenmore Hotel. The man was reported to have left Albany after turning down a bribe he had been offered to testify that he had been massaging Diamond's partially paralyzed left arm at the time Parks was attacked.[175]

A Murder and a Kidnapping

On July 20, state troopers and New York City detectives raided White's Farm, north of Cairo, New York, in Freehold. Eight suspects, alleged to be "foes" of Jack Diamond, were arrested. These alleged members of Vincent Coll's gang (and therefore enemies of both Dutch Schultz and Jack Diamond) were found with an arsenal of "two machine guns, seven sawed-off shotguns, and ten revolvers" with ammunition. Because the gang was apprehended not far from Diamond's summer home, there was speculation that they had come to kill the Diamond gang members and take over Diamond's "beer and rum monopoly" in the area. However, the police could not confirm that this was the reason for the Coll gang members' presence. Three women were among those in the house when it was raided.[176]

On August 27, the *Times-Union* reported that Legs Diamond, who had been "ousted from New York City, Greene County, and Europe," was staying in the Albany home of a friend. Two of Diamond's own bodyguards were reported stationed outside the house in Westland Hills, "one of Albany's most exclusive sections." Diamond's move to this private home on Clermont Street, just off Western Avenue, was attributed to the fact that he had been denied a room at the Kenmore Hotel, where he usually stayed. Since he was on bail and couldn't be put out of town as an undesirable, Chief Smurl's men were reported to have him under surveillance. Diamond was on bail while he appealed a federal conviction that carried a four-year prison sentence. He was also waiting to go on trial again.[177]

In September 1931, New York State Attorney General John Bennett sought tough new anti-gang measures. In a letter sent to both political parties, he requested new laws that would prevent gang members from circumventing the criminal justice system by using strategies such as getting stays, venue changes and bail. Bennett also wanted a measure that would "force advance revelation of an alibi defense" to prevent perjury by defense witnesses. Finally, he wanted judges and prosecutors to have greater leeway in how they conducted trials. Bennett said that his concern about the alibi defense grew directly out of the "surprise alibi" that Legs Diamond had used during his first assault trial in Troy.

Even as attempts were being made to deal with the ability of Diamond to evade conviction, efforts to finally convict him continued. The police had been looking for his mistress, Kiki Roberts. On October 9, she took a taxi to the police station at Watervliet and surrendered. She had been the subject of a police search because she was charged with aiding Diamond and the other gang members in the beating and torture of Grover Park, the Greene County truck driver. Roberts, who arrived at the police station with her suitcase, claimed she had been in hiding because she feared for her safety.

After being arraigned, she was freed on bail. Two months later, Roberts was with Legs Diamond on the last night of his life.

That evening, Diamond, his wife Alice and some friends went out to a speakeasy in Albany to celebrate Diamond's acquittal in Troy for the kidnapping of James Duncan, the second alleged victim in the cider truck incident. Then, leaving his wife and friends, Diamond went to visit Kiki Roberts, who was staying in an apartment on Ten Broeck Street. Diamond then went by chauffeur-driven car to a place that he thought was safe. On the morning that he died, Diamond was sleeping alone in the rooming house at 67 Dove Street. Two men entered his room and shot him three times in the back of the head.

After shooting Diamond, the two men escaped in the car in which they had arrived. According to a newspaper report, the Albany police arrested two photographers who were taking pictures at the scene. Photos of the building and of Legs Diamond's body being removed did later appear in the local newspapers. The newspapers reportedly also served as an early source of information for police departments outside of Albany. Apparently, the Albany police did not immediately send out teletype information about Diamond's murder. However, Chief Smurl and District Attorney Delaney announced soon after that they believed Diamond had been killed by other gangsters.

During the days that followed, Delaney took a trip to Boston to interview Kiki Roberts, who had gone home to her mother. Ms. Roberts's account of her relationship with Diamond—she said she had planned to end it—and what had happened that night was dissected in the newspaper coverage. She was reported to have changed certain details of her story.[178] But Kiki Roberts was not the focus of the investigation. One of the prime suspects in the Diamond killing was Edward "Fats" McCarthy.

In July 1932, Fats McCarthy was killed in Colonie, near Albany, during a gun battle with the police. Officers had hidden in the grass near the cottage where McCarthy was lying low. The cottage had been rented a couple of months earlier by George Kelly, one of McCarthy's gang. During the gun battle, Mrs. McCarthy, who was also staying in the house, was wounded. After the battle, she was taken to the hospital. The police announced their intention to question Mrs. McCarthy and gang members George Kelly and Mike Basile about the murder of Legs Diamond. They were also interested in finding out what the trio knew about the machine gun fire in Harlem the summer before that had left five-year-old Michael Vengali dead. This was the murder generally attributed to New York City gangster Vincent Coll. The *Albany Evening News*, in a headline that was also an epithet, wrote,

A Murder and a Kidnapping

"McCarthy Ends Third Chapter in Lives of State Gang Leaders." The other two chapters were the assassinations of Legs Diamond and Vincent Coll, who had been "Erased by Enemies First."[179]

The murder of Jack "Legs" Diamond remains an unsolved crime. The assumption was that he had been killed by a rival gangster. William Kennedy is a former Albany newspaperman, whose acclaimed "Albany cycle" of novels includes *Legs* (1975), the fictionalized account of Diamond's last days as told by his attorney. In his informal history of the city, *O, Albany!* (1983), Kennedy devoted a chapter to Diamond's death. Considering the suspects, Kennedy notes that Fats McCarthy, whose real name was Edward Popke, was "one of Jack's late-blooming allies (along with Vincent Coll, a psychopathic Irishman)." At the time of Diamond's death, both McCarthy and Coll were hiding in the area. They were wanted by the New York City police on murder charges.

Kennedy relates that one of his sources, a man who worked with gangster Dutch Schultz, claimed that Schultz had assigned Coll and McCarthy to kill Diamond. Instead, they had found Diamond much more likable than Schultz and switched allegiance. Another source, who was in McCarthy's gang, assured Kennedy that McCarthy "absolutely was not involved" in Diamond's murder. Kennedy tended to believe this source. Kennedy notes that one "persistent rumor" about Diamond's murder was that it was carried out by "a death squad from the Albany Police Department." Kennedy observes, "I always thought that was unlikely—why would Albany bother?" But then, looking at the hypothesis more closely, Kennedy notes that Diamond had just "beaten the state's best case against him." He had also announced his intention of "going into business in Albany."[180]

When Kennedy had an opportunity to speak with Dan O'Connell, the still powerful head of the Democratic machine in Albany in 1974, O'Connell was "unusually candid." He mentioned Dan Prior, Diamond's friend and attorney, who "brought Diamond around once too often" to see O'Connell. According to O'Connell, Chief of Police Smurl was too afraid of Prior to take action against Diamond. But William J. Fitzpatrick, an Albany detective who would succeed Smurl as Chief of Police, was not afraid. He had a meeting with Diamond in Troy, during which Fitzpatrick warned Diamond that he would "kill him if he didn't keep going" (leave Albany).

Another source that Kennedy describes as having been involved in the bootlegging business in the 1920s told Kennedy "a parallel story, with some different specifics." According to this source, Diamond had planned to go into the beer business locally with John and Francis Oley. The three planned to try to take over the beer business in Albany. Diamond was arrested on a minor charge while staying at a rooming house on State Street. He was put out of his rooming house and told not to come back. But he did after his acquittal in Troy.

According to a source "close to the Oley brothers before and during this period," John Oley may have killed Legs Diamond. Kennedy observes that "[t]his has been a theory for years." Another theory was that the Oley gang told the police where Diamond was staying in Albany. According to a friend of Diamond's, only his family was supposed to have known where he was staying that night.

Was Legs Diamond's killer Fats McCarthy, John Oley, William J. Fitzpatrick—or someone else? The case remains one of the intriguing unsolved mysteries of gangster history.[181] And it was linked, by way of the Oley brothers, to another crime in Albany that made national headlines. Two years after Legs Diamond's murder, Dan O'Connell and his family were at the center of a high-profile crime that received massive local coverage and national attention as well.

THE KIDNAPPING OF JOHN O'CONNELL JR.

On July 31, 1933, Governor Herbert H. Lehman delivered a message about kidnapping to the New York Legislature. He introduced recommendations for immediate action by stating, "It has become increasingly apparent during the last few months that something must be done to cope with the menace of kidnapping." Lehman went on to outline what he saw as steps to deal with this crime. He recommended that: (1) it be made a felony to agree to pay or to pay ransom; (2) it be made a felony to refuse to divulge information to the authorities; (3) no one be allowed to excuse himself from testifying on the grounds that he might convict himself of a crime (even though he would not be prosecuted on basis of this testimony); (4) prosecutors be required to bring the indicted person to a speedy trial; and (5) the penalties on conviction of kidnapping when the victim was killed be increased from ten to fifty years in prison to twenty-five years to life imprisonment, or death, at the discretion of the jury. With the exception of the provision that would have made paying the ransom demanded by kidnappers a felony, Lehman received the bill that he requested.

The case that prompted Lehman's urgent call for legislative action was the kidnapping of John J. "Butch" O'Connell Jr. The victim was the son of "Solly" O'Connell and the nephew of Democratic Party boss Dan O'Connell. On July 2, 1933, John O'Connell was abducted from in front

A Murder and a Kidnapping

A view of the home of John J. O'Connell Jr., July 12, 1933. *Courtesy of the* Times-Union.

Another view of the home of John J. O'Connell Jr. *Courtesy of the* Times-Union.

of his family home at 14 Putnam Street as he returned from an evening out with his girlfriend, Mary Fahey. John weighed 225 pounds and was an athlete and a lieutenant in the National Guard.[182] But, as he later testified, one man had held a gun on him, and after a scuffle with several other men, he was forced into a car. His mouth and eyes were bandaged. Eventually, the car stopped, and he was put into a crate and onto a truck. He was taken to a room where he was held for days by his captors.

O'Connell's kidnapping came fifteen months after the March 1, 1932 kidnapping of the son of aviator Charles Lindbergh and his wife, Anne Morrow Lindbergh. In fact, the O'Connell kidnapping would later be linked to the Lindbergh kidnapping in various ways. The kidnapping of the Lindbergh's infant son received massive media coverage. One of the most admired men in the country and his wife, also a favorite with the public, waited to see if their child would be returned. Charles Jr. ("the Eaglet") had been taken from his bed. A ladder was found leaning against the wall of the house. The police believed it had been used to climb up to the second-story nursery window. A note was found on the windowsill of the nursery demanding $50,000. The New Jersey State Police was contacted and took charge of the investigation, and the media surrounded the Lindbergh estate near Hopewell, New Jersey. They reported what was known, as well as rumors. They also focused on the fears and hopes of the young parents, Colonel and Mrs. Lindbergh.

As Lindbergh looked for a go-between who could deliver the ransom to the kidnappers, a second ransom note increasing the demand to $70,000 arrived in the mail. The governor of New Jersey called a conference of all of the police officers, prosecutors and other officials working on the case. Lindbergh's attorney hired private investigators. Another ransom note arrived on March 8, rejecting the go-between that Lindbergh had proposed. Then, a retired Bronx schoolteacher, Dr. John F. Condon, offered to serve as the go-between and to add $1,000 of his own money to the ransom. Lindbergh accepted Condon's offer of assistance. Two days later, Condon began negotiating with the kidnappers for delivery of the ransom using newspaper columns and his code name, "Jafsie."[183]

After receiving several more notes, Dr. Condon met a man named "John" in the Woodlawn Cemetery in New York City. After discussing payment, the unidentified man agreed to provide proof that he had the baby. On March 16, a baby's sleeping suit was sent to Condon. Lindbergh identified it as the sleeping suit his son had been wearing when he was kidnapped. The frustrating negotiation through ransom notes continued. So did the search for the child.

A Murder and a Kidnapping

Reports abounded about sightings of the kidnappers with the curly-haired child, whose description was now familiar to newspaper readers. The report that the kidnappers might be headed toward upstate New York or the Canadian border had local and state police officers on the alert. Several days after the kidnapping, the Albany Police Department received a teletype from the state police at the Hawthorne barracks who were relaying information they had received from New York City. According to a tip from a fortuneteller, the child was being brought to Albany by a man named "Peter the Barber." The child's blonde hair was said to have been dyed. Acting on this tip, the Albany police raided a house at Trinity Place. The house was searched and the families there questioned. Drawn by the police sirens, a crowd gathered outside and had to be dispersed. Nothing was found, but Police Chief Smurl left a guard on duty at the house.[184]

Weeks went by without a break in the case. Then the baby's nurse, Betty Gow, found the thumb guard the baby had worn near the entrance to the Lindbergh estate. The next day, on March 30, the ninth ransom note, demanding $100,000, arrived in the mail. A tenth note on April 1 instructed Dr. Condon to be ready to deliver the money the next night. Another note followed. Finally, following the instructions in the twelfth note, Condon met with "John" again and arranged to reduce the ransom to $50,000. Condon was given a receipt and instructions about where to find the baby on a boat near Martha's Vineyard, Massachusetts. A search for the boat and the baby yielded nothing.

On May 12, 1932, the body of Charles Lindbergh Jr. was discovered by accident by an assistant on a truck. The child's body was "partly buried and badly decomposed, about four and a half miles southeast of the Lindbergh home." The examination by the coroner revealed that the baby had been dead for about two months. He had died from a blow to the head.[185]

During the search for the baby, the New Jersey State Police had been the agency in charge. However, A. Henry Moore, the governor of New Jersey, had asked other cities and the federal government to send representatives to a meeting in Trenton. J. Edgar Hoover, director of the Bureau of Investigation (later the Federal Bureau of Investigation or the FBI) was the federal representative. Now, after conferring with the United States attorney general, Hoover contacted the New Jersey State Police to offer Colonel H. Norman Schwarzkopf (father of the general) the Bureau's assistance in apprehending the kidnappers.[186]

When the Lindbergh baby was kidnapped, the federal government had no jurisdiction in kidnapping cases. This was about to change. In 1932, the Federal Kidnapping Act, popularly known as the Lindbergh Law, was enacted. This statute brought kidnapping with the intent to collect ransom or reward under the jurisdiction of the United States government. In September 1933, President Roosevelt requested that the Lindbergh investigation be centralized in the Department of Justice. By October, the Bureau of Investigation had been given exclusive jurisdiction to handle the federal aspects of the case, which included the search for the marked bills that had been delivered to the kidnappers.[187]

The appearance of 296 ten-dollar gold certificates and 1 twenty-dollar gold certificate from the ransom money in the Federal Reserve Bank of New York and the examination of the ransom notes by handwriting experts offered leads in the case. Dr. Condon also provided transcripts of his conversations with "John" that were analyzed for information about the kidnapper's background. The broken ladder thought to have been used by the kidnapper was reassembled to look for information about the maker. Then, on September 18, 1934, an assistant manager at the Corn Exchange and Trust Bank Company reported receipt of a ten-dollar gold certificate. The bill was traced back to a gasoline station. The attendant remembered the man who had given him the certificate. He had been suspicious of the certificate and recorded the man's car license number on the bill. Based on this license number, the suspect was identified as Bruno Richard Hauptmann.

Hauptmann's home in the Bronx was placed under surveillance. Hauptmann was arrested that same day. His description fit that given by Dr. Condon of "John" and by the gas station attendant of the man who had given him the gold certificate. A German immigrant and a carpenter, Hauptmann had been in the United States eleven years. Hauptmann admitted to making purchases with the gold certificates. He denied kidnapping the Lindbergh baby. Based on witness identifications, testimony of handwriting experts and other circumstantial evidence, Hautpmann was tried and convicted of the kidnapping and murder. He was sentenced to death.

The trial, which took place in Flemington, New Jersey, lasted five weeks. That small town became the center of a media circus, with reporters from all over the world arriving to cover the case. The presence of cameras in the courtroom became a matter of controversy that would continue to be debated. Courtroom procedure and the fairness of the trial also became matters of controversy.

As did the rest of the country, Albanians observed this mass media coverage and the outcome of both the kidnapping itself and the trial of Hauptmann. Governor Lehman had signed the extradition papers that sent Hauptmann to New Jersey to stand trial. The next year, when John O'Connell Jr. was kidnapped, the rumors about why he was abducted and who was responsible drew on both the Legs Diamond murder and the Lindbergh kidnapping. According to an article in *Time* magazine published on July 24, 1933, a little over two weeks after O'Connell was abducted, the kidnapping might also have had a Prohibition angle. Recalling the other ransom kidnappings that had occurred in recent years around the country, the magazine suggested that gangsters had moved into the kidnapping racket. In the case of "Butch" O'Connell, there might be added incentive because his uncles were "the unchallenged bosses of Albany," and Butch was the "hope & pride of the clan O'Connell."

Aside from the ransom the kidnappers expected to receive, the crime might represent revenge on the part of beer runners in Albany. The Hedrick Brewery had been back in legal operation since April 7, 1933. Butch O'Connell managed distribution at the brewery that was partly owned by his uncles. The kidnapping might have been payback on the part of the beer runners because Hedrick helped put them out of business. Or it might be related to the threats that "Solly" O'Connell, Butch's father, had received recently. According to the *Time* article, Solly, a Republican who became a Democrat when his brothers took over the Democratic machine, frequented racetracks and raised gamecocks, and his "chief interest now appear[ed] to be sport." The magazine did not speculate about the possible source of the threats against Solly O'Connell. However, as in the local newspaper coverage, *Time* discussed the apparent lack of cooperation of the O'Connells with either the local police department or the agents from the Department of Justice who had been sent to Albany. The O'Connells could do this, *Time* said, because "in Albany their word is law."

When the O'Connell kidnapping occurred, both Governor Lehman and President Roosevelt responded. Federal agents were sent to Albany not only because of the political importance of the O'Connell family, but also because of the mandated involvement of the Bureau of Investigation in such investigations in the aftermath of the Lindbergh baby kidnapping the year before. It was now assumed that kidnapping might cross state lines, making the crime a federal offense. J. Edgar Hoover sent the agent in charge of the New York City office to Albany and ordered the use of the Bureau's facilities in the search for both abductors and victim. Hoover said that the first objective of the law enforcement effort was to "bring about the safe return of Mr. O'Connell." The second objective was "the apprehension of the kidnappers."[188] New York City police detectives also were sent to assist in the investigation. These were the same detectives who had been assigned to trail Vincent Coll, Fats McCarthy and Jack Diamond when the New York City gangsters were hiding out or operating around Albany. The New York

Ransom note from the O'Connell kidnappers addressed to "Dan," July 19, 1933. *Courtesy of the Albany County Hall of Records.*

Above left: Ransom note, undated, addressed to "Dan" from "Roma." *Courtesy of the Albany County Hall of Records.*

Above right: A note from John J. O'Connell Jr. including information about kidnapping codes. *Courtesy of the Albany County Hall of Records.*

State troopers working on the O'Connell case also had been involved with the earlier investigations.[189] But the O'Connells' retreat to their camp in the Heldeberg Mountains and their apparent intent to pay the kidnappers a ransom complicated this investigation.

The note that the O'Connells had received from their nephew said that the kidnappers wanted $250,000 for his release. The kidnappers provided instructions about how the O'Connells should go about finding a go-between who would deliver the money. Placing a newspaper ad, the O'Connells sent a list of names using a code in which the letters of the names were spelled out in numerals. By July 16, 1933, Albany District Attorney Delaney was publicly expressing his irritation with the O'Connell family's "utter lack of cooperation" with law enforcement. He complained that the authorities had "nothing to work on" because the family refused to talk to officials or to turn over the kidnappers' letters.[190] However, as the negotiations continued, Delaney was equally uncommunicative with the press about what was happening, expressing his reluctance to jeopardize any negotiations between the family and the kidnappers that might be underway.

As the investigation continued, Governor Lehman, disturbed by the possibility that the O'Connells or any family might pay a ransom, delivered his message in a special session of the Legislature. He focused on the epidemic of kidnapping and the need to respond in a way that did not encourage such crimes. As this discussion went on in the Legislature, the police agencies involved followed up on tips. They also carried out a raid on a house in New York City in search of O'Connell. The coded messages between the family and the kidnappers continued to be exchanged in the classified sections of New York City newspapers. When the first list of go-betweens was not approved, the family placed a second list of names in the Albany *Times-Union*. When the kidnappers demanded a third list, an ad was placed in another newspaper. From this third list, Manny Strewl (also appears as Strewel or Stroll) was selected by the kidnappers as the go-between. Strewl met with Dan O'Connell and then enlisted the support of an Albany attorney, Louis Snyder.

Unable to raise the sum requested, the O'Connells gave Strewl a bag containing $42,000 (including marked bills). Strewl and Snyder went down to New York City for the meeting. Leaving Snyder to wait, Strewl went to deliver the ransom. He gave the kidnappers only $40,000. Later, there was some discussion about the intent of the other $2,000. Strewl eventually returned it to the O'Connells, minus the ten dollars or so he had in expenses. The kidnappers released John O'Connell on a street corner in the Bronx. He had been held for twenty-three days, much of that time in an apartment in New Jersey. Now, Strewl and Snyder received instructions to bring him to the family "camp" in the Heldeberg Mountains (twenty miles west of Albany). Snyder drove O'Connell to the camp in his car.[191]

The case took an unexpected twist when Manny Strewl arrived at the O'Connell camp and discovered District Attorney Delaney and a police officer waiting to take him into custody. Strewl was accused of being one of the kidnappers. The lists that the O'Connells had been required to post were said to have been a ruse. Both Strewl and Snyder, the lawyer whose help he had enlisted, denied any part in a conspiracy. During the grand jury hearing, Snyder volunteered to testify, but Strewl was convicted and sentenced to prison.

At his appeal hearing, Strewl was represented by Daniel Prior, the friend and lawyer of Legs Diamond. In his opening statement before the court, Prior referred to his client as "this boy" in the same way that the prosecutor referred to John O'Connell Jr. as a "boy." In the narrative that Prior presented to the court, Strewl had not sought involvement in the O'Connell matter. He had received a letter asking him to serve as go-between. He had

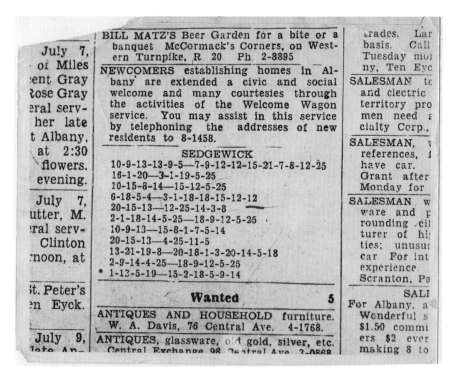

A newspaper ad—possible kidnapping code. *Courtesy of the Albany County Hall of Records.*

John J. O'Connell Jr., in his
National Guard uniform.
Courtesy of the Times-Union.

been surprised but agreed to meet with Dan O'Connell, who asked for his help as a favor to his family. Strewl had agreed but, concerned about his involvement, had sought the support and counsel of Snyder, a respected local lawyer and family man. Throughout the process of recovering O'Connell from his kidnappers, Strewl had acted in good faith. He had persuaded the kidnappers to take less money than they had asked for when they had threatened to send one of O'Connell's fingers or ears to his family. Strewl had returned the $2,000 that the O'Connells had given him to cover expenses. He had never sought any reward for himself. Strewl was, his attorney said, a boy who was the victim of a frame-up. Prior said that his client had been abused by the Albany police, who had held him incognito until his lawyer obtained a writ of habeas corpus requiring that Strewl be brought before a magistrate. When Strewl appeared, he still had a black eye from the beating that he had received days earlier.[192]

When Prosecutor Delaney made his opening statement to the appellate court, he offered a decidedly different narrative of events. In this version, Strewl was not an innocent boy, but a clever criminal. According to the prosecutor, the police and the O'Connell family had suspected early on that Strewl might be involved. He had been placed under surveillance. Seeming to become aware of the surveillance, he had contacted the lawyer, Snyder. He had also asked for a meeting with Dan O'Connell. O'Connell had assured him that everything was fine and that he should continue his negotiations. The prosecutor raised the question of whether Strewl had intended to give back the additional $2,000 that had not been passed on to his conspirators or if he had only done so when asked about the money during questioning by the police.[193]

Strewl would continue to appeal his sentence. It was almost four years before the police finally believed that they had all of the members of the "ring" that had been involved in O'Connell's kidnapping. As his case continued through the criminal justice system, John O'Connell married Mary Fahey, the young woman with whom he had been out on a date on the night he was kidnapped.

The murder of Jack Diamond in Albany and the kidnapping of a scion of the powerful O'Connell family marked the end of a turbulent era. As the country settled into the Great Depression, the exploits of gangsters and the fates of their victims were perhaps secondary to the concerns many people were feeling about how they and their families would survive.

Chapter 4

PROHIBITION ENDS, DEPRESSION BEGINS

The Stock Market Crash of 1929 was not the only cause of the Great Depression, but it symbolized for many Americans the moment when the good times of the 1920s ended. Not all Americans had seen their incomes rise during the 1920s. Some groups, such as farmers, coal miners and small merchants who had been put out of business by chain stores, had not shared the economic prosperity of the 1920s.[194] But for those who had seen their standard of living rise in the 1920s and dreamed that life would only get better, the "hard times" of the 1930s were hard indeed. In Albany, by the early 1930s, "total wages fell over 27 percent and the city was aiding 2,200 families with fuel, food, and rent assistance."[195]

The federal government, under President Roosevelt, would initiate numerous assistance programs during the Depression. At the local level, private charities and organizations also played a crucial role in the relief effort. In Albany, Trinity Institution, a settlement house in the South End, provided services to those in need. Salvation Army units across New York State were involved in collecting clothing and other salvageable articles that were donated for the homeless. At the same time, the Salvation Army offered food and shelter to the homeless who helped to repair and distribute the items that had been collected. In Albany, the J.B. Lyon Printing Company donated a building to the Salvation Army. The "Lyon Lodge" became a "model institution" that was praised by the mayor and the commissioner of public welfare. First Lady Eleanor Roosevelt toured the facility. However, the Lodge "was designed primarily to serve the local homeless." Transients passing through Albany could "stay only on a temporary basis."[196] Among the private agencies, Travelers Aid continued in its mission of providing assistance to persons in transit. Referrals

Excavation for the construction of Trinity Institution, May 7, 1928. *Courtesy of Albany Institute of History & Art Library.*

Construction of Trinity nearing completion, October 16, 1928. *Courtesy of Albany Institute of History & Art Library.*

Feeding children at Trinity Institution. *Courtesy of Albany Institute of History & Art Library.*

were made to other agencies, such as the YMCA, YWCA and the Salvation Army, in Albany and other cities.[197]

Federal efforts to provide relief to transients were underway. In August 1933, the *Knickerbocker Press* reported that the "Weary Willie" camps—gathering places for "itinerant travelers"—were being dispersed as jobs became available through New Deal programs. Only two such "jungles" (camps), occupied by "professional 'bos" (hoboes), remained in the vicinity of Albany. One was at the end of the Erie Canal basin, at the foot of Erie Street in North Albany. The other was a quarter of a mile from Putnam Street. However, even as some men found employment, others remained homeless. On January 10, 1936, the *Albany Evening News* observed that the "hundreds of penniless, homeless, and wandering men on Albany streets are the 'forgotten men' in the present relief situation."[198]

During the Depression, there were at least two groups of homeless: (1) those who had become unemployed and lost their homes because of the Depression and (2) those who were rootless and unattached for reasons that were more personal than economic. Historic concerns about those without ties to the community were enhanced by the times. Vagrancy laws were one means of controlling the itinerant population. These laws also provided police officers with a mechanism for taking suspicious persons into custody while conducting further investigation.

Salvation Army, 63 Liberty Street. Note the sign indicating an office of employment, prisoners' aid and missing friends, 1936. *Courtesy of Albany Public Library.*

In March 1931, two vagrants were arrested by New York State Trooper Edward C. Updyke. He suspected that they might have been involved in a holdup the day before. Their car had a Pennsylvania license, and the men had silk shirts, shoes and other clothing in the car. When they were committed to the Rensselaer County Jail in Troy while the authorities investigated the ownership of the car and checked for criminal records, Updyke and Sergeant John E. Frey headed to Troy with the two men. Frey was driving the men's car with one of the suspects. Updyke was behind him in a police car with the other suspect as a passenger. On the Troy–New York Road near East Greenbush, Updyke turned a corner and saw the suspect who had been riding with Sergeant Frey standing in the road pointing a gun. Updyke stopped and was forced to surrender his car to the two men. As he was starting for help, he came across Frey's body. The two suspects abandoned the stolen car near the riverfront in Rensselaer. Then they crossed the bridge and disappeared into Albany.[199]

On January 3, 1932, the *Knickerbocker Press* described "a new gangsterism" in Albany. It was nothing as violent as the murder of Sergeant Frey by the two "vagrants," but this perception of a new form of gangsterism did involve homeless men. In this case, the men were the victims. According to the report of a narcotics agent, homeless men were being given shelter in the backrooms of speakeasies. In exchange, the men were being forced to go out and panhandle and then use the money to buy cheap rum from the speakeasies where they were lodging.[200] This was the Albany, in the grip of the Great Depression, that novelist William Kennedy wrote about in *Ironweed* (1984).

The plight of the down-and-out in Albany was also captured in a small item that appeared in the *New York Times* in January 1936. A Philadelphia woman who had not been seen by her family since 1932 was found dead in a basement apartment in Albany. She had once been a dancer in a burlesque company, but four years earlier the company had been stranded in Albany. She had stayed, taking a job as a nightclub hostess. She died of acute alcoholism. The man with whom she had shared the apartment told police that they had not eaten for the three days before her death. He was arrested for vagrancy, but his sentence was deferred for a week.[201]

When the Depression came, the federal government was slow to respond. President Herbert Hoover seemed to some Americans to lack empathy for their loss of jobs and homes. This seemed particularly the case in the summer of 1932, when the "Bonus Army," thousands of veterans of World War I and their families and supporters, came to Washington, D.C., seeking early cash payment on the service certificates the veterans had received.

Prohibition Ends, Depression Begins

The marchers set up camp in shacks on Anacostia Flats. When they refused to leave their "Hooverville," the military, under the command of General Douglas MacArthur and Major George Patton, went into the area with bayonets drawn. Hooverville was destroyed and the Bonus Army routed.

This action and other indications that Hoover lacked sympathy for Americans in need propelled Franklin Delano Roosevelt, former governor of New York, into the White House. Roosevelt had campaigned on the promise of a "New Deal." He believed that the federal government should intervene with economic and social programs to alleviate the impact of the Depression. Roosevelt had already experimented with prototypes of some of these programs while he was governor of New York. He believed that it was the state's obligation to take responsibility for the welfare of its citizens. As an industrial state, New York experienced almost thirty-five hundred factory closings between 1929 and 1933.[202] New York had enacted the 1929 Public Welfare Law, which provided an apparatus that many other states failed to provide for the poor. However, there were aspects of the law and how it was administered that made it difficult for some of the poor, such as transients, to receive aid. Even before he took on the task of dealing with poverty in the country as a whole, Governor Roosevelt found himself confronted by citizens of New York who said the response of the state was too little and too slow.

Governor Franklin Delano Roosevelt congratulates Admiral Byrd in 1930. Eleanor Roosevelt applauds the event. *Courtesy of Albany County Hall of Records.*

Protest and Riot

On February 26, 1931, Communists rallied in Union Square in New York City. They were about to begin a march to Albany.[203]

On March 3, 1931, headlines in the *Times-Union* proclaimed: "Troopers Club Reds in Capitol, Riot Free-For-All Battle in Assembly" and "Many Injured as Mob of Jobless Overpowers and Pummels Police Guard."

Many of the "Reds" who were involved in the battle with New York State troopers were reported to have come to Albany for the protest. There was, however, a local office of the Communist Party in Albany. The office was located on Central Avenue. A small item that appeared on June 28, 1931, in the *Times-Union* reported that the police, who had until then ignored the Saturday night open-air speeches by the Communists, had this time made arrests. None of those arrested were able to make bail.[204]

The riot that occurred at the Capitol began when William J. Johnstone, the leader of the protest, requested and was denied the opportunity to read his petition on the floor of the New York State Assembly chamber. Two New York State troopers who tried to remove Johnstone from the balcony were surrounded by angry protestors. The police officers drew their guns to hold the crowd off, but they were overpowered. Other state troopers rushed to the balcony, and a riot erupted with both clubs and fists flying. The protestors were taken into custody.[205]

In July 1931, ten men identified as Communists attempted to pass out handbills on Herkimer and Pearl Street. About 130 men had gathered there in response to an advertisement for 50 workers. Men were needed as strikebreakers in White Plains, where streetcar workers were on strike. The Communists opposed both the kind of work being offered and the wages being paid. The next month, in August 1931, a group of unemployed men and woman "attempted to stage a demonstration" at the Capitol in Albany. Having advance warning, the police stopped them on the steps, keeping them out of the building. Twenty-five state troopers and ten Albany patrolmen were involved in the encounter. Five people were arrested and taken to the Second Precinct. The *New York Times* reported, "Albany Police Club Red Group at Capitol."[206]

When the protestors came back to Albany in November of the following year, Governor Franklin D. Roosevelt tried a different strategy. He agreed to meet with the leaders of the "hunger marchers" and received them in his study in the Executive Mansion. The protest leaders presented the governor with four demands: (1) appropriation of $100 million in immediate relief to help the unemployed; (2) opening of all armories in the state to the homeless; (3) provision of food and transportation for the hunger marchers to Washington, D.C.; and (4) a guarantee that the marchers would not be molested by law enforcement in New York cities along the way. The governor said no to all of these demands. However, he explained that $15 million was now available to the state, and another appropriation for the same amount was pending. Roosevelt said that he would open the armories to the homeless and unemployed if he received word from mayors that the local facilities were insufficient. He could not legally authorize the use of state trucks to transport the marchers. Nor did he have jurisdiction over the police, although he assured the marchers that they had the right to travel. He hoped the police would use "humane methods and give them fair treatment."[207]

The Albany police also developed a strategy for dealing with the marchers. In March 1933, the police simply escorted the three hundred men and women who had come to Albany up Capitol Hill and back down again. Onlookers lined the street to see the parade as the delegates of the Workers Conference for Labor Legislation passed by. Police officers were on either side of the marchers, and Police Chief Smurl led the way in his car. Meanwhile, state troopers guarded the entrances to the Capitol to ensure that none of the marchers got inside. There was "no disorder."[208]

But the next year, the *New York Times* reported, "Albany 'Brutality' Arouses Protests." Representatives of civil liberties and workers' groups went to see Governor Lehman at his home in New York City. They were there to protest the alleged brutality that the Albany police had used in breaking up a "hunger march." Two hundred unemployed marchers had scuffled with the police when they tried to enter the Capitol. Many were reportedly injured, and sixty-five were arrested. Governor Lehman, echoing Roosevelt, pointed out that the city police were outside his jurisdiction. He, too, recognized the marchers' right to peaceful assembly and assured them that he would be glad to receive them at his New York City office.[209]

As governor, Roosevelt demonstrated some empathy for those who were in need. In fact, many of the programs he later introduced as president had their prototypes in New York State. This included the Civilian Conservation Corps (CCC), said to be his favorite of his federal New Deal programs. As president, Roosevelt created numerous agencies and implemented programs, including the Works Progress Administration (WPA) and CCC. In Albany, WPA projects were as varied as the murals in the building that is now the University at Albany Dewey Library and the Hawk Street Viaduct.

The Civilian Conservation Corps program focused on men between the ages of eighteen and twenty-four (later eighteen to twenty-five) who applied to the program. They went into the mountains, national parks and other

Workers pour hot asphalt over bricks to resurface the Hawk Street Viaduct in 1933. Projects like these were aided by the Federal Program, Works Progress Administration. The city sponsored the cost of materials and equipment, while the federal government sponsored the labor costs. *Courtesy of Albany County Hall of Records.*

locations to engage in conservation activities. Under the supervision of military officers, the men lived in barracks or camps. They wore uniforms, and they did kitchen patrol. The men earned thirty dollars a month. Twenty-five dollars was automatically sent home to support their families. Even so, five dollars and lodging, food and clothing made the CCC appealing during a time when the alternative for the young men and their families might be bread lines. A number of the camps were located in New York State, drawing men from Albany and other cities. The CCC seems to have had another effect that was not widely discussed by Roosevelt or other supporters of the program. By enlisting young men from ages eighteen to twenty-four, the program might also have served a crime-prevention function. It removed young males (a crime-prone group) from urban settings during an economic crisis when they might well have been more likely to engage in crime.[210]

Roosevelt and the Prison Riot

While governor of New York, Roosevelt had shown some interest in criminal justice and law enforcement policy. However, although reform-minded, he had also been cautious. He was a governor with his eye on the presidency.

Prohibition Ends, Depression Begins

Roosevelt had taken a tough stance on organized crime. However, his critics argued that crime continued to flourish in Albany. Toward the end of his term as governor, he was criticized for what Republicans described as the failures of his administration. When a riot occurred at Clinton Correctional Facility in Dannemora, New York, his political opponents argued that the riot had been "avoidable." They claimed that the riot was the direct outcome of the breakdown of three state agencies: prison, banking and public works. His opponents criticized Roosevelt for his failure to make maximum use of housing units at Clinton to relieve the overcrowding.[211] Governor Roosevelt responded that the additional housing units at Clinton had not been fit for human occupation. He argued that the stringent Baumes laws, which gave some prisoners no hope of release, and the inadequate prison buildings had been important factors in the riot. In a special message to the Legislature in Albany, he discussed the riots. The day before Roosevelt's scheduled speech, the Crime Committee, which had sponsored the Baumes laws, offered a number of bills aimed at responding to the Clinton riot. Included was a prison building project and increased pay for prisoners.[212]

Regarding the prison riot, the *New York Times* reported, "Penologists Blame Concentration of Desperate Convicts at Clinton." These prisoners were "lifers" who were said to have nothing to lose. Three had been killed during the riot. On September 13, 1929, the *New York Times* reported that wardens and others were telling President Roosevelt that improvements in the prisoners' living conditions were essential. These experts advised that the prisoners be served better food. They also advised that the prison population not exceed the housing limit of fifteen hundred.[213]

When it came to Prohibition, Roosevelt had been reluctant to adopt the "wet plank" that called for repeal of the amendment. As a presidential candidate, he adopted the wet position of his party. Although Hoover, Roosevelt's opponent in the upcoming election, had called Prohibition a "noble experiment," even he acknowledged that it was not working well. Hoover appointed a presidential commission, the National Commission on Law Observance and Enforcement, known as the Wickersham Commission. Headed by George W. Wickersham, the commission had eleven committees charged with examining various subfields of crime and law enforcement. The commission submitted its final report on January 10, 1931.

The findings of the commission were contradictory. Although a majority of the members believed that Prohibition had failed, the commission recommended that it continue. At the same time, the commission documented the corruption and abuse that had characterized Prohibition law enforcement. These findings and the deepening Depression, which required the federal government's resources, provided Roosevelt and Congress with adequate justification for repealing the Eighteenth Amendment (with enactment of the Twenty-first Amendment).

WICKERSHAM COMMISSION ON LAW ENFORCEMENT

The findings of the Wickersham Commission about police corruption and brutality generated another kind of controversy. Based on its investigation, the commission concluded that one of the byproducts of Prohibition had been an increase in police corruption. At the same time, the commission criticized the methods used by police in obtaining statements and confessions from suspects. Of particular concern was the "third degree" used in interrogations. The suspect was subjected to long periods of questioning under stressful conditions, such as bright lights and lack of food, water and sleep. The commission cited fifty such cases that it had discovered during its investigation. Charles Doran, the Albany man who had been executed for his participation in the robbery and murder of an Albany filling station owner, was one of those cases.

A headline in the August 10, 1931 *Times-Union* stated, "Albany 'Third Degree' Method Hit." The newspaper reported that the Wickersham Commission had found that in the Doran case, the Albany police had exceeded their "legal power" when they arrested Charles Doran (and his two alleged accomplices). The men were not taken before a magistrate, but held in custody without warrants and taken to another city. Doran was held for over a week without arraignment. During this time, he and his alleged accomplices were taken to Watervliet, a neighboring city. There, Doran was questioned and confessed to District Attorney Delaney (at the time an assistant District Attorney) and Assistant Police Chief Peacock.[214]

The questioning of Doran took place in the police gymnasium. During the interrogation, Peacock was alleged to have been wearing a boxing glove. District Attorney Delaney denied the Wickersham Commission's finding that Doran had been subjected to third-degree methods, which had led to his confession. Delaney said that he was present during the interrogation and the police had not abused Doran.[215] This claim by Doran's defense attorney did not succeed during the trial. The court of appeals confirmed Doran's conviction, noting that "numerous witnesses" contradicted his claim of abuse. By the time the Wickersham Report was released, Doran—who was executed—had been dead for several years.

The Wickersham Commission made an argument about appropriate police behavior that would not be incorporated into the criminal justice process for another three decades. In the 1960s, the United States Supreme Court handed down a series of decisions, including *Miranda v. Arizona*, which established the rights of a suspect now familiar to every viewer of television crime shows. In the Prohibition era, it had not yet been established that a suspect should "have the right to remain silent…and to have a lawyer appointed if you cannot afford one," etc.

From the standpoint of the police, the Prohibition era presented special problems in law enforcement related to the huge profits to be made by engaging in bootlegging, racketeering and other forms of organized crime. Police officials actively lobbied for legislation that they thought would lead to more effective law enforcement. For example, in March 1933, Police Commissioner Mulrooney from New York City came to Albany to appear before a joint hearing of the senate and the Assembly Codes Committee. Mulrooney came to express his objections to a "model" pistol bill that would eliminate the fingerprinting and photographing of upstate applicants for pistol permits. The Commissioner told the legislative committee that such a change in the law would allow New York City gangsters to obtain guns upstate. He pointed to the case of gangster Salvatore Spitale, who had obtained an upstate permit from a county judge despite the fingerprint provision. When he was made aware of Spitale's criminal background, the judge revoked his permit and those of the two other gangsters who had also obtained permits. Commissioner Mulrooney also reminded the Committee of the assassination attempt on President-elect Roosevelt in Florida by Italian immigrant and self-described anarchist Guiseppe Zangara. The would-be assassin had purchased his .38-caliber pistol at a Miami pawnshop. Mulrooney argued that it was more important than ever to keep guns out of the hands of criminals. Assemblyman Edmond, the chairman of the committee, suggested that if Florida had the kind of model legislation that was being proposed in Albany, then Zangara would have been required to wait forty-eight hours while his identification was being checked before he could have purchased the pistol. Assemblyman Edmond also pointed out that gangster Dutch Schultz had been able to buy a gun in Suffolk County (downstate, Long Island) despite the present law.[216]

As president, Roosevelt expanded the role of the federal government with social and economic programs. He also created the conditions that would allow the expansion of federal law enforcement—Hoover's FBI. Although he disapproved of some aspects of the agency, Roosevelt used the Bureau for surveillance activities. He also gave the agency full rein in the "war on crime." This was another aspect of Roosevelt's broader effort to extend federal power "to yet another realm, crime control." President Roosevelt believed that the crime problem posed "a legitimate threat to 'our security.'" He also was dismayed by the tolerance the American public showed for Depression-era gangsters, who were often seen as romantic folk heroes. Both matters seemed to call for New Deal reform. At the same time that Roosevelt and United States Attorney General Homer S. Cummings promoted the expansion of the jurisdiction of federal law enforcement, anticrime bills were being sent to and passed by Congress.[217]

Lehman's "Little Deal"

Following Roosevelt as governor of New York, Herbert Lehman also followed the president in adopting certain programs. Lehman's approach has been called the "Little Deal" (echoing Roosevelt's New Deal). When it came to crime, Lehman focused on organized crime at the state level. In May 1935, he signed the "Public Enemy" Act (the Brownell Bill). This act barred criminals from consorting. It also created a new state criminal investigation service (an American version of Scotland Yard) by decentralizing the investigatory services of the state police.[218] In October 1935, Lehman backed a law to fingerprint everyone as a weapon against crime.[219]

These actions on the part of Lehman and the Legislature came at a time when the governor was being accused of being lax on crime. That July 1935, the Republicans had called on Lehman to investigate the O'Connell brothers in Albany after Lehman appointed District Attorney Thomas Dewey to investigate crime and racketeering in New York City.[220] That fall, Walter Mahoney, president of the New York State Young Republican Club, called the conference on crime that Lehman convened in Albany a preelection stunt, a "grand gesture." Mahoney said that Lehman was refusing to initiate an investigation of crime in Albany and Erie Counties.[221] Lehman's conference on "crime, the criminal, and society" had taken place the month before in September. Raymond Moley, who had prepared the report on crime for President Roosevelt, was among those presenting at the four-day conference.[222]

Reverend George Drew Egbert, the president of the Society for the Prevention of Crime, echoed Mahoney, the Young Republican, in his criticism of Lehman. In a sermon delivered that October in a church in Queens, Egbert accused the governor of "permitting 'outrageous' vice and crime conditions to flourish" in Albany. He, too, challenged the governor to initiate an investigation. Egbert said that agents of the society had found "wide open" houses of prostitution in Albany. One, he alleged, was within two blocks of the Capitol. Prostitutes were also soliciting on the streets. As for gambling, the agents had gathered policy slips and advertising material. When the governor was given the material, he said that he would turn it over to the Albany District Attorney. But Egbert implied that this was unlikely to go anywhere because the half brother of the District Attorney had represented defendants in Albany during the federal baseball pool investigation.[223]

Other organizations were also concerned about crime, but often with broader agendas. In 1931, members of the National Women's Party had come to Albany to support the Jenks Bill. This bill proposed to hold men "equally guilty with women for prostitution." The members of the Women's Party expressed their concern to the Assembly Codes Committee that the Seabury Investigation had found that members of the New York Police Department vice squad sometimes "framed" innocent women for prostitution.[224] In November 1935, the State League of Women Voters held its sixteenth annual convention in Albany. The League decided to initiate an active campaign for the prevention of juvenile delinquency. Juvenile delinquency was an issue that Governor Lehman also considered important. In a speech to another group, the Albany Woman's Club, he advocated the use of psychiatrists in schools. He argued that these trained professionals would be able to identify youths with problems and help to prevent delinquency. He told his audience that improving the criminal justice system was a matter of small steps. During his administration, Lehman continued to push his crime-fighting agenda.[225]

The state Legislature had its own concerns about crime, among them a topic that is still debated today. During the 1930s, there was increasing concern among Americans about sexual predators. In August 1937, the Legislature decided to began an inquiry into sex crimes. In what was intended to be "an exhaustive investigation," the legislators wanted to determine whether parole policies had contributed to what was perceived as a "recent wave of sex crimes against children."[226] By December 1937, at least one group had demanded stricter laws for sex offenders. Thomas D. Scoble, chairman of the Westchester County Citizens Committee, appeared before the Joint Legislative Committee on Law Enforcement to ask for "broad statutory reforms to curb sex offenders," who he described as "potential murderers."[227]

ALBANY GEARS UP TO RESPOND TO CRIME

In Albany, one response to crime in the 1930s was to enhance facilities and acquire new equipment for the police department. In September 1931, the new Albany County Jail opened. With the old building in disrepair and outdated, a new jail was needed. Located on Shaker Farm and built at a cost of $1 million, the new jail was described by the *Times-Union* as "one of the finest penal institutions in the country."[228] Annual reports to the Commissioner of Public Safety detailed police purchases and upgrades to police facilities. In 1931, Chief Smurl reported that the department had acquired eight Essex roadsters and one Essex sedan. The sedan would be assigned to the detective "office." Each of the six precincts would receive a roadster as a prowl car. The captain of traffic would receive a roadster, and one would be held on reserve for emergencies and as a replacement when a precinct car needed repairs. Chief Smurl also reported on the new spring and fall "double-breasted blouse" that had been established for use in the department. The City of Albany had paid half of the cost for the new uniform addition.[229]

The 1932 report included a description of the renovations and additions to the First Precinct station house. The station house could now accommodate twenty male prisoners. A cell room with accommodations for two female prisoners and a matron's room had also been added.[230] In 1933, purchases by the police department included "six Remington 11-R-12 gauge shot guns and ammunition for same," as well as "6 Thompson Sub-Machine U.S. Navy model 1928 machine guns and ammunition." The officers had been instructed on their use. That year, three more cars—Essex Terraplane roadsters—were acquired. This allowed each precinct to have two prowl cars in service.[231] In 1934, a radio broadcasting station was established, enhancing police communication.[232]

Built in 1846, the old county jail stood behind the present Hackett Junior High School and Albany Veterans Administration Hospital. It was torn down in 1931, when the new Albany County Jail was erected on the site of the Old Shaker Farms in Colonie. *Courtesy of Albany County Hall of Records.*

However, even as new aspects of crime and crime fighting (such as how to respond to sex offenders) claimed the attention of lawmakers, the police and the public,[233] two Albany crime sagas continued.

CONTINUING CRIME SAGAS

By August 1937, all of the eight members of what the federal government called "the last organized crime ring" had been convicted by a federal jury. These were the men who had taken part in the kidnapping of John O'Connell Jr. back in 1933. The ring included three Albany natives: John Oley, Percy Geary and Manning Strewl, who had served as the go-between during the ransom negotiation. As participants in this conspiracy, the eight men in the ring received sentences ranging from twenty-eight to seventy-seven years in prison and fines of $10,000 each. Strewl received a sentence of fifty-eight years; Oley and Geary each received seventy-seven years. O'Connell, who was now twenty-eight years old, testified during the eleven-week trial. During this trial, 172 prosecution and defense witnesses testified. The jury reached its decision after three hours of deliberation.[234]

But this was not the end of the O'Connell kidnapping case. On November 18, 1937, the *New York Times* reported: "Two Hunted Kidnappers Are Trapped in Syracuse." Three members of the kidnapping ring had escaped the day before from Onondaga Penitentiary at Jamesville, New York, where they had been imprisoned pending their appeals. The ringleader of the escape had been Albany native Percy "Angel Face" Geary. After a massive police search, Geary, John Oley and Harold "Red" Crowley were located in a rooming house in Syracuse. The janitor had tipped the police that they were there. Geary managed to escape out a window as the police officers were using a key to enter the locked bedroom. Oley and Crowley surrendered and were taken into custody. When the room was searched, two revolvers were found under the bed.

The State Commission of Corrections[235] investigated how the men had managed to escape and found "a number of discrepancies in the different stories" that they heard from the guards and officials at the prison. Albany native John Oley said that they had gotten the guns after the escape. He said they had used tobacco pipes to fool the guards. He said Geary had found a cell bar loose and torn it out, then put it back into place with chewing gum. However, Oley observed, "These local cops are lots smarter than G-men." Although he considered Geary "the smartest of them all," he was confident that he would see him at Alcatraz. The three men faced an extra five-year

In 1938, the Ritz Theatre ran a double feature, *Prison Break* and *One Wild Night*. Some people preferred to shop at one of the several stores on South Pearl Street near Howard. *Courtesy of Albany County Hall of Records.*

sentence for the breakout. Four of the other men involved in the conspiracy were already serving time at Alcatraz.[236]

As for Manny Strewl, he had his sentence reduced to twenty-two years in prison. This happened in October 1938, when the United States Circuit Court of Appeals, in a decision written by Judge Learned Hand, quashed three of the five counts against Strewl. The convictions that were quashed were those of mailing extortion letters from New York City to Albany and two letters in Albany.[237]

Three of the men involved in the O'Connell kidnapping conspiracy committed suicide while incarcerated. In 1937, Christopher Miller, a native of Hoboken, New Jersey, hanged himself in the Albany County Jail. That same year, Francis Cley, who was an Albany native, hanged himself in the Oneida County Jail. In 1938, George Romano hanged himself in the state prison in Charlestown, Massachusetts. Romano was facing two long sentences for robberies committed in Massachusetts, in addition to the seventy-seven-year sentence he had received in the O'Connell case.[238]

The other continuing crime saga also involved the O'Connell family. Even as World War II approached, calls were still coming from the Republicans for an inquiry into alleged criminal activities in Albany County. In November 1938, Senator Thomas C. Desmond of Newburgh joined New York City District Attorney Thomas E. Dewey, who was now running as the Republican candidate for governor, in demanding an investigation. Desmond said that he would sponsor a legislative investigation. In his campaign speeches, Dewey had "singled out Albany County as a center of 'crime in politics.'" In a radio address in October 1938, Dewey began by saying that Albany was a "political racket, a political monopoly" run by the O'Connell machine.

Dewey repeated the accusation made by others that in Albany, grill and tavern owners were being forced to buy their beer from Hedrick Brewery, the O'Connell's company. The consequences of not buying Hedrick's beer, Dewey said, was that the saloon owner would have "every rule in the book against him." According to affidavits Dewey had received, those who tried to resist the Hedrick's monopoly found that they had to close at 1:00 a.m., while saloons buying Hedrick's beer stayed open all night. They also found that they had trouble getting their licenses renewed. Dewey said that in Albany, Hedrick's beer was "the only beer on draught in 200 out of 258 grills and taverns."[239]

During this radio address, Dewey also commented on the O'Connell kidnapping. He said that when the O'Connells had been asked to provide names of men who might serve as possible go-betweens in the ransom negotiation, they had no problem generating thirty names for the three lists they had provided. These were men "named for the underworld to do business with." Dewey identified several of the men on the list as members of the Democratic organization headed by the O'Connells. The O'Connells, Dewey said, headed a "political machine filled with racketeers." Dewey expressed his confidence that most Democratic voters would be pleased to see the O'Connell machine broken. This machine, he said, was too much for "any man"—including a Democratic governor—to cope with and must be tackled by "the people" with their vote.[240] Dewey made a special plea to women to register to vote in the upcoming election and to encourage their family members to do the same.[241] Dewey lost in a close election. In 1942, he ran again and was elected governor. Dewey's election did not bring an end to the O'Connell Democratic machine.

Epilogue
LOOKING BACKWARD

It is a cliché to say that the more things change, the more they remain the same. But looking back at Albany in the 1920s and '30s from the perspective of today, it is striking how many issues of that era remain relevant. As historians have pointed out about the country as a whole, the war against crime during the Prohibition era, when the focus was on gangsters and bootleggers, has its parallel in the late twentieth-century war against gangs and drug dealers. During each era, there was the reality of crime. There also was the mythmaking about "the crime fighters" and "the bad guys" that helped to shape the public discourse about "violent crime" and what should be done about it.

In the last decade of the nineteenth century, sociologist, historian and civil rights activist W.E.B. Du Bois described the neighborhoods in which African Americans lived in *The Philadelphia Negro* (1899). As he and later sociologists of the Prohibition era documented, segregation was not restricted to the South. As black migrants arrived in Northern and Midwestern cities, they settled in those areas in which they were allowed to rent or buy housing. Although they sometimes lived in racially and ethnically diverse neighborhoods, over time their white neighbors tended to move out as more blacks moved in. Hindered by the housing stock available to them, African Americans found themselves paying higher prices for inadequate housing in neighborhoods where they received limited municipal services.

In the nineteenth century, white European immigrants, particularly the Irish, lived in wretched tenements in the poor, crime-infested neighborhoods. They were the focus of both public contempt and reformers' efforts. They were also stigmatized as violent, criminal and dangerous. By the early twentieth century, African Americans living in poor inner-city neighborhoods had inherited this burden. In Albany, in a 1928 report, the National Urban League found that the African American population was small. In the 1920 census, African Americans accounted for only 1,239 out of a total population of 112,344.[242] The Urban League investigation found that the "principal areas occupied by Negroes" in Albany were:

> *Area I. Church to Pearl Streets; Hudson to Schuyler*
> *Area II. Broadway to South Swan; Monroe, Van Tromp, Orange and Sheridan*
> *Area III. The vicinity of Spencer and Jackson Sts., and Broadway*
> *Area IV. First to Lexington Avenue—Ten Broeck to Northern Boulevard*[243]

The report noted, "In these areas only a few of the blocks are wholly Negro, while the white neighbors are heterogeneous in character, being chiefly foreign born." Area I, where both blacks and "a proportionately large foreign born" population lived, was in the South End. This was the location of the "red-light district," identified years earlier in the place where vice crime flourished. Their presence in this area meant that African Americans found themselves under greater police surveillance than the residents of other Albany neighborhoods.

At the same time, the Urban League report found that although "a relatively small number of Negro children appear before the children's court there is every indication that certain untoward conditions exist in the immediate environment which are conducive to crime." The conditions noted in the "vicinity bounded by Division, Church, Pearl and Herkimer Streets" included: (1) the "'red light' district under constant surveillance of the Police Department" but with little suppression of "commercialized vice"; (2) "the open playing of 'policy' ('the numbers')" in this area; and (3) the presence of a men's rooming house section, occupied by "homeless men, casual laborers" and "the haven" of those seeking "anonymity."[244]

In the end, it was urban renewal that destroyed "the Gut." Among these renewal projects was the Empire State Plaza, the complex of state office buildings, state museum and state library built during the administration of Governor Nelson Rockefeller. Urban renewal displaced both the residents of downtown neighborhoods and the areas in which vice crime in Albany had flourished. However, reports of crime, drugs and violence in Albany that appeared in local newspapers in the 1920s and '30s still appear on a daily basis in the local media. The police still occasionally propose new strategies

Sheridan Avenue, northwest corner, near Swan Street, 2008. The building to the right of the church is now the site of the Interfaith Partnership for the Homeless. A homeless shelter now sits in back of the church. *Photograph by Alice Green.*

for dealing with the crime problem in Arbor Hill and the South End, the areas where crime in Albany is reported to be concentrated. These are still areas where poor and working-class people—now predominantly people of color—live.

Perhaps the most significant change is that, today, conflicts between the police department and citizens about policing, police misconduct and how to improve relations between the community and the police department are often addressed through a citizen's review board. However, the discussion about the role of race in Albany police–community relations can be traced back to the 1930s. In 1935, when the Albany chapter of the National Association for the Advancement of Colored People (NAACP) was founded, its primary goals were "equal access to housing, education, employment, and an end to police brutality."[245]

In Albany (as in the rest of the country), the issue of how to respond to crime is still debated. One of the solutions proposed by the New York Senate Crime Committee in the 1920s was the Baumes laws that focused on the incapacitation of offenders. The "four times and you're out" legislation that sent fourth-time offenders to prison for life served as a model for other states during the Prohibition era. This approach would have a late twentieth-century parallel in the "three strikes and you're out" legislation in California

This page: During Prohibition, many of the inhabitants of this area were Irish-Americans; now, many of the residents are African Americans. Many of the buildings are in disrepair or abandoned. *Photographs by Alice Green, 2008.*

and elsewhere. However, soon after the Baumes fourth offender legislation was enacted, critics such as Warden Lawes of Sing Sing and Governor Franklin Roosevelt were pointing out that many of the people being caught up in the Baumes net were petty offenders, not the violent criminals that the law had been intended to take out of circulation. Moreover, as Roosevelt pointed out after the Clinton prison riot, prisoners without hope for eventual release and an overcrowded prison system were a dangerous combination.

By the 1930s, the New York Senate Crime Committee was taking another look at the Baumes laws in the wake of the problems that arose. New York began moving toward indeterminate sentencing. With the enactment of the stringent Rockefeller drug laws in 1972, New York returned to an approach with echoes of the Baumes laws. The mandatory sentencing required by the Rockefeller drug laws led to mass incarceration of low-level offenders rather than the drug kingpins. After years of calls for repeal of the Rockefeller drug laws that sent thousands of men and women to prison and disrupted families, the Legislature made some modifications in the state drug laws. Yet, over the past twelve years, there has been a significant drop in the numbers of people being released on parole. As in the 1920s and '30s, this would suggest more of a focus on punishment than on rehabilitation and reintegration of the offenders into the community. As with the Baumes laws, those with little hope of parole have limited incentive for good behavior.

What is also striking is that New York State in the 1920s experimented with releasing first-time prisoners after they had served half their sentences. Ironically, notorious gangster Monk Eastman, who had been a model prisoner, was one of the beneficiaries of this law. However, even Eastman apparently managed to go straight for several years before becoming involved in another holdup. Today, the discussion continues about whether those serving their first sentence (who generally have far fewer encounters with the police than Eastman prior to incarceration) should be treated differently than repeat offenders. Many criminal justice experts argue that long sentences for first-time prisoners, particularly nonviolent offenders, may be counterproductive if the goal is to return the prisoner to the community as a law-abiding citizen.

Finally, any look backward should include politics in Albany. What is fascinating about the 1920s and '30s is the accusation about the corruption and criminality of the Albany Democratic machine led by Dan O'Connell. In spite of O'Connell's brief incarceration related to the Albany baseball pool, he survived as the boss of the Albany machine, and the machine remained entrenched. Thomas Dewey, who had campaigned as a crusader against the O'Connell machine, was unable to overthrow it when he was elected governor. Even with the deaths of Dan O'Connell and his political ally, Erastus Corning, who served as mayor of Albany for forty-two years, the machine continued. In recent years, some significant cracks have appeared as candidates who were not handpicked by political powerbrokers have been elected to the District Attorney's office, the Common Council and the school board (an independent body but still influenced by machine politics). These insurgents have challenged traditional party candidates and won. However, Albany remains staunchly Democratic, with Democrats outnumbering Republicans nine to one. Some Albanians would argue that although the machine may not be as strong as it was during its glory days, it still exercises influence over both local politics and the administration of state government. The relationships that exist among the governor, state legislators and Albany politicians remain crucial to the city and its development. Albany is still the place where decisions that affect all New Yorkers are made.

As William Anderson of the Anti-Saloon League observed in 1914, New York City's influence was far-reaching. As he soon realized, Albany was the less glitzy seat of power where decisions about New York City were being made. Anderson came to Albany to battle for Prohibition. He won that battle, but his victory was only temporary. Then, as now, Albany resisted change.

Albany remains a fascinating city. Its historical importance is often underestimated, even by Albanians. For those who wish to understand the present, it is worth looking backward at Albany, New York, during the Prohibition era. The more some things change, the more they *do* remain the same.

Appendix A
LIST OF GOVERNORS AND ALBANY OFFICIALS

GOVERNORS OF NEW YORK, 1919–54

(Note: Until 1938, New York governors served two-year terms.)

Alfred ("Al") Smith (Democrat, January 1, 1919–December 31, 1920)
Nathan L. Miller (Republican, January 1, 1921–December 31, 1922)
Alfred ("Al") Smith (Democrat, January 1, 1923–December 31, 1928)
Franklin D. Roosevelt (Democrat, January 1, 1929–December 31, 1932)
Herbert H. Lehman (Democrat, January 1, 1933–December 3, 1942, resigned to accept post in U.S. Department of State)
Charles Poletti (Democrat, December 3, 1942–December 31, 1942)
Thomas Dewey (Republican, January 1, 1943–December 12, 1954)

MAYORS OF ALBANY, 1919–41

James R. Watt (Republican, 1918–21)
William S. Hackett (Democrat, 1922–26, died in office)
John Boyd Thacher II (Democrat, 1927–40, resigned)
Herman F. Hoogkamp (Democrat, 1941, completed Thacher's unexpired term)
Erastus Corning II (Democrat, 1941–83, died in office)

APPENDIX A

ALBANY COMMISSIONERS OF PUBLIC SAFETY
(1919–39)

J. Sheldon Frost (1917–21)
James T. Keith (1922–25)
Frank Lasch (1926–30, died in office)
William V. Cooke (1930–36)*

*On March 14, 1936, the Department of Public Safety was abolished, and the Department of Police, with a Commissioner of Police, was created. James A. Kirwin assumed the position of Commissioner of Police. (Proceedings of the Common Council Reports, November 1, 1936).

ALBANY CHIEFS OF POLICE (1919–40)

James L. Hyatt (1901–retired December 31, 1921)
Frank Lasch (1922–retired August 28, 1926)
David Smurl (September 16, 1926–1940)

Appendix B

LOCATIONS OF POLICE PRECINCTS (1922)

First Precinct, Arch and Broad Streets

Second Precinct, Howard and Williams Streets

Third Precinct, North Pearl Street between Livingston Avenue and Wilson Street

Fourth Precinct, Madison Avenue below Lark Street

Fifth Precinct, Central Avenue above North Lake Avenue

Police Headquarters: Offices of the Chief of Police, detectives and police justices were located in the Second Precinct. A new building was under construction at the corner of Beaver and Eagle Streets.[246]

NOTES

Newspaper articles for which no page number appears were found in the Police Scrapbooks (on microfilm) in the archives of the Albany County Hall of Records.

CHAPTER 1. 1919

1. *Times-Union*, "Insulted, Girl Beats One Man, Routs His Pals," August 19, 1919, 1.
2. Lisa S. Strange and Robert S. Brown, "The Bicycle, Women's Rights and Elizabeth Cady Stanton," *Women's Studies* 31 (2002): 609–26. See also Ellen Gruber Garvey, "Reforming the Bicycle: Advertising-Supported Magazines and Scorching Women," *American Quarterly* 47, no. 1 (1995): 66–101.
3. James R. Chiles, "Hallelujah, I'm a Bum," *Smithsonian* 29, no. 5 (1998): 66–74.
4. Dominick C. Lizzi, *Governor Martin H. Flynn* (Valatie, NY: Valatie Press, 2007).
5. *New York Times*, "Barnes Belittles Albany Exposure," October 15, 1911, 13.
6. *New York Times*, "Osborne to Direct Albany Inquiry," September 6, 1911, 1; *New York Times*, "Albany Dodges Law of Competitive Bids," November 3, 1911, 6.
7. *New York Times*, "Barnes Dodges All Political Questions," October 25, 1911, 9.
8. *New York Times*, "Barnes Need Not Answer," January 17, 1912, 2.

9. *New York Times*, "Accept Albany Vice Report," March 30, 1912, 2.

10. *New York Times*, "Albany Vice Report Rejected by Senate," May 29, 1912, 1.

11. *New York Times*, "Rejoice at Barnes Defeat," May 23, 1915, 14.

12. *Times-Union*, "The Barnes Machine 'Smashed' the Women of Albany in 1917—The Women Will 'Smash' the Barnes Machine in 1919," October 1917, 1.

13. *Albany Evening Journal*, "At 91 Mrs. Alvira Carter Feels it is Her Duty to Vote Republican Ticket," 1919.

14. *Times-Union*, "Looking for a Big Police Upheaval," February 28, 1919.

15. *Times-Union*, "Puzzled," July 16, 1919.

16. *Times-Union*, "Albany Police Want More Pay: Talk of Strike," September 5, 1919, 1.

17. Francis Russell, *A City in Terror: 1919, The Boston Police Strike* (New York: Viking Press, n.d.)

18. *Times-Union*, "Hope of Reinstatement Lost to Boston Police," September 17, 1919, 1; *Times-Union*, "Police Given New Hope By Commissioner Frost," September 17, 1919, 1.

19. *Times-Union*, "De Forest Murder was Deliberate," July 9, 1919, 1; *Times-Union*, "Investigate Men Who Knew Mrs. De Forest," July 11, 1919, 1; *Times-Union*, "Men Loitered near House of De Forest," July 14, 1919, 1.

20. *Times-Union*, "Robbers Work Boldly; Man and Woman Held Up," October 17, 1919, 1.

21. *Times-Union*, "Girl Says Gang of Young Men Broke into Her Room," January 30, 1919, 1. See also *Times-Union*, "Gangsters Take Girls to Their Clubs," January 4, 1919, 1; *Times-Union*, "Police Will Break up Gang of Loafers," January 31, 1919, 1.

22. *Times-Union*, "It's a Harvest Town, Say the Busy Crooks," October 2, 1919, 1.

23. *Albany Evening Journal*, "Here's the Way to Treat E'm Rough," February 14, 1919.

24. *Albany Evening Journal*, "Girl Attacked Near Wolfert Roost Club," March 12, 1919.

25. The newspaper referred to here was not the *Times-Union*, which was an evening newspaper.

26. *Albany Evening Journal*, "Hasty Criticism of the Albany Police," January 31, 1919, 3.

27. *Albany Evening Journal*, "Dignified, Lucid, True," October 1, 1919, Editorial, 6.

28. *Albany Evening Journal*, "The Record is the Best Promise," October 4, 1919, Editorial; *Albany-Evening Journal*, "Futile Slander," October 4, 1919, Editorial.

29. *Times-Union*, "Captain Townsend Albany's Next Mayor," November 4, 1919, 1.

30. *Times-Union*, "Election Earthquake Rocks G.O.P. Machine," November 5, 1919, 1.

31. *Albany Evening Journal*, "Campaign of Vilification," November 1919.

32. *New York Times*, "Barnes Sells Paper to Political Rival," February 6, 1925, 19.

33. Michael A. Lerner, *Dry Manhattan: Prohibition in New York City* (Cambridge, MA: Harvard University Press, 2007).

34. Ibid.

35. Scott McCloud, "Origins of the Early Albany Temperance Movement" (master's thesis, School of Social Work and Behavioral Sciences, University at Albany, 1993).

36. *Times-Union*, "'No Beer, No Work,' Slogan of Labor Men," February 26, 1919, 1.

37. *Times-Union*, "Police Chief Sees Spread of Drug Habit," January 30, 1919, 2.

38. *Times-Union*, "Breweries Are Ready to Start Again," January 25, 1919, 12.

39. Lerner, *Dry Manhattan*.

40. Ronald Allen Goldberg, *America in the Twenties* (New York: Syracuse University Press, 2003).

41. *Times-Union*, "Textile Girls Lectured by Judge Brady," March 3, 1919, 1.

42. *Times-Union*, "Strike Here Looms as Shopmen Take Vote," August 7, 1919, 1.

CHAPTER 2. THE ROARING TWENTIES

43. *New York Times*, "Drug Package Sent to Senator," March 28, 1923, 1.

44. *New York Times*, "Ascribe to Klan Attack on Smith," March 1, 1923, 1.

45. *New York Times*, "Seeks Injunction against Klan," July 25, 1923.

46. *Times-Union*, "Police Guard Buildings in Sacco Crisis," August 11, 1927.

47. For discussion of these cases, see Frankie Y. Bailey and Steven Chermak, eds., *Famous American Crimes and Trial*, vol. 3 (Westport, CT: Praeger, 2004).

48. For discussion of this case, see Frankie Y. Bailey and Donna L. Hale, *Blood on Her Hands: The Social Construction of Women, Sexuality, and Murder* (Belmont, CA: Wadsworth, 2004), 129–33, 242–43.

49. In fact, Edgar Allan Poe's C. Auguste Dupin was the first fictional detective to capture the public imagination in three short stories. However, he was surpassed in fame by Doyle's Holmes, whose adventures continued into the twentieth century and who was later immortalized in film and on television.

50. For discussion, see David E. Ruth, *Inventing the Public Enemy: The Gangster in American Culture, 1918–1934* (Chicago: The University of Chicago Press, 1996).

51. Gerda W. Ray, "From Cossack to Trooper: Manliness, Police Reform, and the State," *Journal of Social History* (1999): 565.

52. Ibid., 570–71.

53. New York State Police, *The First Fifty Years, 1917–1967* (N.p., n.d.).

54. Ray, "From Cossack to Trooper," 573.

55. Ibid., 573.

56. Victor J. Di Santo, *The Streetcar Workers of Albany, 1900–1921: The Union Era* (Ann Arbor: University of Michigan, n.d.), v.

57. Ibid., iv.

58. Ibid., 240.

59. Ibid., 297–99.

60. *Times-Union*, "Avert That Street Car Strike," January 27, 1931, 4; *Times-Union*, "The Public Be Damned," January 31, 4.

61. *Knickerbocker Press*, "Police Prepared on Chief's Order for Long Strike," January 29, 1921.

62. *Knickerbocker Press*, "Chief Hyatt Sets 15 Cents as Limit for Jitney Fares," January 31, 1921.

63. *Knickerbocker Press*, "Fifty Policemen Ordered to Guard Car Barns," February 3, 1921.

64. *New York Times*, "Trolley Strike On in 5 Upstate Cities," January 29, 1921.

65 .*Times-Union*, "The Public Be Damned," January 31, 1921, 4.

66. Di Santo, *Streetcar Workers of Albany*, 302.

67. Ibid., 304–5.

68. Ibid., 306–7.

69. *Albany Evening Journal*, "Intimidation is Keeping People off Cars, Says Weatherwax," March 14, 1921.

70. *Albany Evening Journal*, "Mayor Watt is Asked to Have the Jitneys Removed," March 18, 1921.

71. *Knickerbocker Press*, "'Criminal Clans Know Handicaps of Police in Tieup Row,' Says Hyatt," March 6, 1921.

72. *Knickerbocker Press*, "Explosion Shatters North Albany Panes: Suspect is Arrested," March 13, 1921.

73. *Albany Evening Journal*, "Session of Grand Jury is Extended to Deal with Traction Situation," March 18, 1921.

74. *Knickerbocker Press*, "Albany Police Take up Eighth Week of Duty in U.T. Strike," March 21, 1921.

75. Di Santo, *Streetcar Workers of Albany*, 309.

76. Ibid., 314.

77. Ibid.

78. Ibid.

79. Ibid., 316.

80. *Knickerbocker Press*, "Business Zone Swept by Worst Strike Riot: 1,000 Storm Trolley," May 20, 1921.

81. *New York Times*, "Albany Rioters Stone Street Cars and Fight Police," May 21, 1921, 1.

82. Ibid.

83. *Knickerbocker Press*, "250 Troopers Called in Albany Crisis; All Will Be Here Sunday," May 22, 1921.

84. *Knickerbocker Press*, "State Police Patrol Streets in Helmets, Armed with Rifles," May 24, 1921.

85. Gerda W. Ray, "We Can Stay Until Hell Freezes Over: Strike Control and the State Police in New York, 1919–1923," *Labor History* 36 (1995): 403.

86. *New York Times*, "Decide Not to Call Troops to Albany," May 23, 1921, 12.

87. Di Santo, *Streetcar Workers of Albany*, 320–21.

88. Ibid., 323.

89. Proceedings of the Common Council Reports, Annual Report of the Chief of Police, 1921.

90. Ibid.

91. *Times-Union*, "Search Local Café, Seize Some Liquid," February 6, 1920, 1.

92. *Argus*, "Two Held after Police Raid Nets Big Liquor Stock," October 21, 1920.

93. Lerner, *Dry Manhattan*.

94. *New York Times*, "'Dry' Act Repeal Passed by Senate," March 28, 1923, 1.

95. *Times-Union*, "Marsh Gives Evidence of Vice to Mayor," January 24, 1923, 1.

96. Proceedings of the Common Council Reports, Annual Police Reports, 1919–33.

97. *Argus*, "Two Men Found Dead," October 21, 1919.

98. *Times-Union*, "Blinded and Crazed," May 28, 1921.

99. *Albany Evening Journal*, "Man is Blinded and Crazed by Prohibition Whiskey," May 27, 1922.

100. *Knickerbocker Press*, "Poison Whiskey Made in Albany at 200 Places," May 28, 1922.

101. *Times-Union*, "Poor Man's Club," June 26, 1920, 11.

102. *New York Times*, "Federal Agents Raid Albany Speakeasies," January 31, 1921, 2.

103. Sean T. Moore, "National Prohibition in Northern New York" (master's thesis, Department of History, University at Albany–SUNY, n.d.).

104. Moore, "National Prohibition."

105. *Times-Union*, "Ale in His Car Brings Arrest of Albany Cop," September 31, 1931.

106. *Times-Union*, "Albany Chinamen, Murder of Tong, Wants Gun Permit," October 22, 1924.

107. *Times-Union*, "Tong Warfare Again; Albany Chinks Cower," November 28, 1924.

108. *Albany Evening News*, "Agents, Cops, Arrest 7 in Opium Raids," August 31, 1931.

109. Proceedings of the Common Council Reports, Annual Police Reports, 1919–24.

110. *Knickerbocker Press*, "Six Albany Pedlars of Drugs Leave for U.S. Atlanta Prison," March 24, 1922.

111. *Times-Union*, "Dope Chief Praised Albany Police Work," March 23, 1923, 1.

112. *Argus*, "Roundup of Undesirables," December 21, 1920; December 23, 1920.

113. *Knickerbocker Press*, "Two New Arrests in Poolroom Used by Drug Peddler," September 20, 1921.

114. *Knickerbocker Press*, "Alleged Drug Agent Jailed in Fifth Raid on Albany Poolroom," September 22, 1921.

115. *Knickerbocker Press*, "Adjacent Drug Crime," September 20, 1921.

116. *Knickerbocker Press*, "Capt. 'Sam' Keith Opens Cleanup in Second Precinct," January 5, 1922.

117. *Knickerbocker Press*, "Police Start Special Night Patrol to End Albany Crime Series," March 30, 1922; *Knickerbocker Press*, April 2, 1922.

118. *Times-Union*, "Albany Cops Fight 'Dope,' Have City in Fine Shape," February 20, 1928.

119. *Knickerbocker Press*, "Pool Rooms Given Sunday Privilege by Hyatt's Order," January 23, 1921.

120. *Knickerbocker Press*, "New Sabbath Order from Albany Police Bans Hotel Dancing," January 27, 1921.

121. *Knickerbocker Press*, "Police Make New Drive to Abolish Giant Ball Pools," August 10, 1921.

122. *Times-Union*, "Albany Hotbed of Gambling Hackett Hears," April 11, 1923, 1.

123. Proceedings of the Common Council Reports, Annual Police Reports.

124. *New York Times*, "Saratoga Springs Told Gambling Must Stop; Gov. Smith Threatens to Oust City Officials," June 5, 1920, 17.

125. *New York Times*, "Gov. Smith Ousts Saratoga Officials," October 1, 1926, 25.

126. *New York Times*, "'Albany Pool Broken,' The Sheriff Reports," May 3, 1925, 26.

127. *New York Times*, "Big Gambling Pool is Under Scrutiny," December 3, 1926, 14.

128. *New York Times*, "36 Are Indicted in Gambling Pool," December 4, 1926, 19.

129. *New York Times*, "Lays Vice in Albany to the Democrats," August 2, 1927, 7.

130. *Albany Evening News*, "Chief Smurl Orders Albany Vice Cleanup," October 8, 1927.

131. *New York Times*, "Roosevelt Assails Smith as 'Quibbler,'" November 7, 1927, 6.

132. *New York Times*, "Three Sentenced in Baseball Pool," July 13, 1928, 11.

133. *New York Times*, "Says Pool Obtain $50,000,000 Yearly," August 1, 1928, 23.

134. *New York Times*, "Smith Attacked on Baseball Pool; Demands Proof," September 9, 1928, 1.

135. *New York Times*, "Roosevelt Witness on Baseball Pool," September 28, 1928, 1.

136. *New York Times*, "Ball Pool Witness, Defiant, is Warned," August 1, 1929, 16.

137. *New York Times*, "Ball Pool Witness, Defiant, is Warned," August 1, 1929, 16.

138. *New York Times*, "O'Connell Arrest Ordered by Court," December 28, 1929, 10.

139. *New York Times*, "O'Connell is Hunted in Canada and Cuba," January 3, 1930, 2.

140. *New York Times*, "Arguments Begun on O'Connell Appeal," January 7, 20.

141. *New York Times*, "Upholds Sentence on D.P. O'Connell," April 8, 1930, 33.

142. *New York Times*, "O'Connell is Jailed in Ball Pool Case," June 14, 1930, 36.

143. *New York Times*, "Roosevelt Demands Baseball Pool End," June 20, 1931, 2.

144. *Albany Evening Journal*, "Armed Cars to Patrol Streets of Albany to Curb Crime," March 29, 1922.

145. *Knickerbocker Press*, "Police Start Special Night Patrols to End Albany Crime Series," March 30, 1922.

146. Proceedings of the Common Council Reports, Annual Police Report, 1923.

147. *New York Times*, "Curbing Speeders on Death's Highway," June 8, 1921, 4.

148. Proceedings of the Common Council Reports, Annual Police Report, 1934, 155.

149. Proceedings of the Common Council Reports, Annual Police Report.

150. *Albany Evening Journal*, "Young Woman is Slain On Division Street by Man with whom She Lived," September 3, 1921.

151. *New York Times*, "Albany Politician Kills His Wife," December 6, 1925, 13.

152. *Times-Union*, "Ex-Alderman Devine Reveals Atrocious Crime in Confession," December 5, 1925; "Mrs. K.G. Barnes, Who is Named by Slayer's Son, to be Questioned."

153. Earl W. Waldron, "'Whitey' Quick to Anger; Doomed to 'Go Down,'" *Times-Union*, February 6, 1928.

154. *New York Times*, "2 Bid Gray Good-Bye, Then Die in Chair," January 6, 1928, 4. See also *New York Times*, "Gov. Smith Indicates He Will Deny Pleas of Snyder Slayers," January 6, 1928, 1.

CHAPTER 3. A MURDER AND A KIDNAPPING

155. *Knickerbocker Press*, "Gangsters Defy 'Cops': Strip One of His Gun; Raid Union Hall Dance," February 18, 1921.

156. *Knickerbocker Press*, "Gangster Arraigned as Pals Crowd Court; One Gets Term in Pen," February 19, 1921.

157. *Times-Union*, "Albany Free Of Organized Crime, Chief Smurl Asserts," August 25, 1931.

158. *New York Times*, "'Legs' Diamond Slain in Sleep at Albany by Two Assassins," December 19, 1931, 1.

159. See *New York Times*, "An East Side Vendetta," September 15, 1903, 8; *New York Times*, "'Monk' Eastman Caught After Pistol Battle," February 3, 1904, 16; *New York Times*, "Lamar Found Not Guilty," October 17, 1903, 6.

160. See *New York Times*, "'Monk' Eastman Will Go to Penitentiary," April 15, 1904, 14; *New York Times*, "Monk Eastman Free on Prison Parole," June 20, 1909; *New York Times*, "Trap Monk Eastman Fleeing in an Auto," May 18, 1918, 7; *New York Times*, "'Monk' Eastman, Gangster, Murdered," December 27, 1920, 1.

161. *New York Times*, "Diamond in Tombs Again, May Get Out," July 16, 1930, 20. In this article, Diamond is said to have been sent to "the workhouse." However, an article on July 18, 1930, titled "Jack Diamond Freed in Newark Hold-up," reports that he was sent to Elmira Reformatory on his one conviction.

162. *New York Times*, "Gangsters Mourn as 'Augie' is Buried," October 16, 1927, 12.

163. *New York Times*, "Gangsters Mourn," October 16, 1927, 12.

164. *New York Times*, "Diamond Queried on Rothstein Case," March 27, 1930, 22.

165. *New York Times*, "Rearrest Diamond after His Release," March 22, 1930, 10.

166. *New York Times*, "Links Slain Gangster with 'Legs' Diamond," April 17, 1930, 13.

167. *New York Times*, "Diamond in Tombs Again, May Get Out," July 16, 1930, 20.

168. *New York Times*, "Jack Diamond Freed in Newark Hold-up," July 18, 1930, 28.

169. *New York Times*, "Diamond Arrested in Albany Hospital," May 5, 1931, 4.

170. *New York Times*, "Gang Tries to Get Diamond's Papers," May 6, 1931, 1.

171. *New York Times*, "Trial of Diamond Will Be Set Today," May 18, 1931, 4.

172. *Albany Evening News*, "Albany Guard Ordered over Jack Diamond," July 9, 1931.

173. *Albany Evening News*, July 10, 1931.

174. *New York Times*, "Diamond Acquitted of Assault Charge," July 15, 1931, 1.

175. *New York Times*, "Seek Clue in Maine on Diamond's Alibi," July 18, 1931, 30.

176. *New York Times*, "8 of Diamond's Foes Seized in His Haunts," July 20, 1931, 1.

177. *Times-Union*, "'Legs' Diamond Living in Westland Hills," August 27, 1931.

178. Roberts's relationship with Diamond and her last evening with him received extensive coverage. See, for example, *New York Times*, "Girl Surrenders in Diamond Case," October 9, 1931; *Times-Union*, "Marion Roberts Revises story of Diamond's Visit to Apartment," December 30, 1931; *Albany Evening News*, "Miss Roberts Tells of Visit with Diamond," December 31, 1931.

179. *Times-Union*, "McCarthy Gang Faces Quiz in Jack Diamond Slaying," July 12, 1932; *Albany Evening News*, "McCarthy Ends Third Chapter in Lives of State Gang Leaders," July 12, 1932.

180. William Kennedy, *O, Albany!* (New York: The Viking Press, 1983), 203.

181. Ibid., 204–10.

182. *New York Times*, "Abducted Last Thursday," July 11, 1933.

183. Federal Bureau of Investigation (FBI), "Famous Cases," http://www.fbi.gov/fbihistory.htm.

184. *Times-Union*, "Albany Police Seek Lost Baby," March 6, 1932.

185. FBI website.

186. *New York Times*, "Police Heads Meet with Moore Today," March 5, 1932, 1.

187. *New York Times*, "Open Fresh Inquiry in Lindbergh Case," October 20, 1933, 1.

188. *New York Times*, "Cummings Sends Agents to Albany," July 12, 1933, 3.

189. *New York Times*, "Lehman Offers Reward," July 12, 1933, 1.

190. *New York Times*, "Delaney Incensed at O'Connell Kin," July 16, 1933, 12.

191. *New York Times*, "O'Connell Captors Force New Agents," July 15, 1933, 1; *New York Times*, "Returns Unhurt at 4 A.M," July 31, 1933, 1; *New York Times*, "Strewl Questioned in O'Connell Case," August 1, 1933; *New York Times*, "Strewl is Jailed in O'Connell Case," August 9, 1933, 8.

192. In the Court of Appeals of the State of New York, *The People of the State of New York v. Manning Strewl* (Albany, NY: The Argus Co. Law Printers, 1936).

193. Ibid.

CHAPTER 4. PROHIBITION ENDS, DEPRESSION BEGINS

194. Kathleen Drowne and Patrick Huber, *The 1920s* (Westport, CT: Greenwood Press, 2004).

195. Jennifer A. Lemak, "Albany, New York and the Great Migration," *Afro Americans in New York Life* and *History* (January 2008): 2. See also Jennifer

A. Lemak, "Southern Life, Northern City; The History of Albany's Rapp Road Community" (PhD dissertation, State University of New York, 2004).

196. Joan M. Crouse, *The Homeless Transient in the Great Depression: New York State, 1929–1941* (Albany: State University of New York Press, n.d.), 83.

197. Ibid., 78.

198. Quoted in Crouse, *Homeless Transient*, 230.

199. *New York Times*, "State Trooper Slain by Prisoners in Car," March 19, 1931, 2.

200. *Knickerbocker News*, "New Gangsterism Rises in Albany among Jobless," January 3, 1932.

201. *New York Times*, "'Missing' Dancer Dies in Albany Hospital," January 9, 1936, 25.

202. Crouse, *Homeless Transient*, 53.

203. *New York Times*, "Reds at Rally Here Ask Cash for Idle," February 26. 1931, 11.

204. *Times-Union*, "Red Arrested, Police Break up Gathering," June 28, 1931. See also *Knickerbocker Press*, "Police Break up Open Air Meeting of Albany Reds," June 28, 1931.

205. *Times-Union*, "Troopers Club Reds in Capitol Riot; Free-For-All Battle in Assembly," March 3, 1931. See also *Albany Evening News*, "Troopers Crush Red Riot in Capitol," March 3, 1931.

206. *New York Times*, "Albany Police Club Red Group at Capitol," August 26, 1931, 2.

207. *New York Times*, "Roosevelt Hears 'Hunger Marchers,'" November 19, 1932, 1.

208. *New York Times*, "Albany Police Divert Unemployed March," March 8, 1933, 7.

209. *New York Times*, "Albany 'Brutality' Arouses Protests," November 1, 1934, 1.

210. For discussion of this aspect of the CCC, see John A. Pandiani, "The Crime Control Corps: An Invisible New Deal Program," *British Journal of Sociology* 33, no. 3 (1982): 348–58.

211. *New York Times*, "Republicans Open Fire on Roosevelt; Attack 3 Bureaus," January 3, 1930, 1

212. *New York Times*, "First Prison Bills Offered By Baumes," January 2, 1930, 3.

213. *New York Times*, "Lay Riot To Excess of Long-Term Men," July 23, 1929, 3. See also *New York Times*, "Prison Experts Argue 1,500 As Housing Limit," September 13, 1929, 25; *New York Times*, "3 Convicts Killed, 20

Hurt, 1,300 Riot at Dannemora, Set Fire and Storm Walls," July 23, 1929, 1.

214. *Times-Union*, "Wickersham Board Raps Doran Case Procedure," August 10, 1931. See also *Albany Evening News*, "Wickersham Group Scores Third Degree," August 10, 1931; *Albany Evening News*, "Brutal Police Action Cited in Doran Case," August 10, 1931.

215. *Times-Union*, "Wickersham Board Raps Doran Case Procedure," August 10, 1931.

216. *New York Times*, "Mulrooney Fights 'Model' Pistol Bill," March 1, 1933, 8.

217. For discussion, see Kenneth O'Reilly, "A New Deal for the FBI: The Roosevelt Administration, Crime Control, and National Security," *Journal of American History* 69, no. 3 (1982): 638–58.

218. *New York Times*, "'Public Enemy' Act Signed by Lehman," May 16, 1935, 19.

219. *New York Times*, "Lehman Backs Law to Fingerprint All," October 3, 1935, 1.

220. *New York Times*, "Eaton Asks Inquiry on Albany Machine," July 24, 1935, 18.

221. *New York Times*, "Lehman Is Accused of Laxity on Crime," October 9, 1935, 8.

222. *New York Times*, "500 Are Expected at Crime Meeting," September 24, 1935, 48.

223. *New York Times*, "Lehman Assailed on Albany Crime," November 18, 1935, 42.

224. *New York Times*, "Women Back Bill for Equal Vice Guilt," March 4, 1931, 7.

225. See, for example, these *New York Times* articles: "Drastic New Laws Urged by Lehman in Drive on Crime," January 8, 1936, 1; "7 More Bills Signed by Lehman," March 7, 1936, 2.

226. *New York Times*, "Legislatures Begin Sex Crime Inquiry," August 20, 1937, 22.

227. *New York Times*, "Drastic Sex Laws in State Demanded," December 3, 1937, 2.

228. *Times-Union*, "Albany County's New Jail," September 2, 1931. See also *Times-Union*, "Closing Order Brings Cell Problem," September 15, 1917.

229. Proceedings of the Common Council Reports, Annual Police Report, 1931, 161.

230. Ibid., 1932, 148.

231. Ibid., 1933, 152.

232. Ibid., 1934.

233. This issue claimed the attention of legislators in 1937, when they voted to launch an inquiry to learn more about sex crimes and determine whether parole methods had contributed to the recent wave of sex crimes against children.

234. *New York Times*, "Eight Convicted in O'Connell Case," August 13, 1937, 38.

235. The authors note here that the investigatory tasks carried out by this agency may have changed and may not be the same as the present agency.

236. *New York Times*, "Two Hunted Kidnappers Are Trapped in Syracuse," November 18, 1937, 1.

237. *New York Times*, "Strewl Sentence Reduced to 22 Years," October 18, 1938, 26.

238. *New York Times*, "O'Connell Kidnapper Suicide in His Cell," March 10, 1938, 3.

239. *New York Times*, "Dewey's Radio Address Assailing the O'Connells," October 25, 1938, 8.

240. Ibid.

241. *New York Times*, "Dewey Condemns Machine in Albany," October 8, 1938, 1.

EPILOGUE. LOOKING BACKWARD

242. Ira Dea Reid, *The Negro Population of Albany, New York: A Survey* (National Urban League, December 1928), Table No. I.

243. Ibid., 10.

244. Ibid., 33.

245. Lemak, "Albany and the Great Migration."

APPENDIX B. LOCATIONS OF POLICE PRECINCTS (1922)

246. *History of the Police Department of the City of Albany New York* (published by and for the benefit of the Albany Police Beneficiary Association, December 1922), 21.

Please visit us at
www.historypress.net